CUSTOMER FIRST

A Strategy for
Quality Service

CUSTOMER FIRST

A STRATEGY FOR QUALITY SERVICE

Denis Walker

Gower

Published by
Gower Publishing Company Limited
Gower House
Croft Road
Aldershot
Hants GU11 3HR
England

Gower Publishing Company
Old Post Road
Brookfield
Vermont 05036
USA

British Library Cataloguing in Publication Data
Walker, Denis
  Customer first.
  1. Companies. Customer services. Management aspects
  I. Title
  658.812

ISBN 0 566 02860 3

Printed in Great Britain by BPCC Wheatons Ltd, Exeter

Contents

Contents

Figures

Acknowledgements

The writing of the book has spanned a considerable period of time. Thanks are due to my wife Miriam (helped by Gwen), who painstakingly typed, amended and corrected my words to the extent where our children are sure it is her book and not mine. I would also like to thank a number of clients who became friends and who helped with the ideas in the book – Robert Gibson, Malcolm James and Bob Mitchell of ICI and Roger Comery from the National Health Service – and Laurie McMahon, a fellow consultant.

Denis Walker

Preface

Customers are the lifeblood of all organizations. Yet few seem fully capable of matching their performances to the needs of their customers, either in quality, efficiency or personal service. Managers must start to recognize that improving quality to their customers is not a matter of choice – the health of the organization depends on it.

The purpose of this book is to show what has to be done to create a total commitment to customers. To illustrate what is possible and how to set about the task, I have drawn on my experience of managing change within British Airways and on my later career as a consultant.

The book is aimed primarily at executives who recognize that to achieve quality improvement coupled with total commitment to customer service a new style of management is required. It is a style based on developing skilled and knowledgeable people at all levels through communication and training, and then using their expertise to seek better ways of doing things. It is a style based on clear standards and targets and the use of data and statistics to drive continuous improvement. It is a style which combines the art of people management with the science of reducing variability.

The book is in three parts. The first part develops the concept of service at a strategic level and offers a template for auditing the service 'health' of an organization. The second part provides practical examples of data capture, training, communication and project activity which can be combined in a dynamic framework for improvement. The examples are intended to stimulate thought and provide a basis for designing your own activities to meet established needs. This part also explores the key elements of managing a service business and shows how excellent service performance can be used as a potent marketing weapon.

The third part tells the story of British Airways from 1983 to 1989. It shows how 'putting the customer first' helped to turn a a rather sickly, slow-to-respond, bureaucratic giant into a competitive, vibrant and customer-responsive organization. It shows the never-ending nature of such programmes and the very broad front across which service and quality improvement has to be attacked. It demonstrates that total quality is not for the faint-hearted or uncommitted, but provides inspiration for those who wish to undertake the journey. The book concludes by demonstrating how worthwhile such an investment will be – for customers, for staff and managers and for all other stakeholders.

Denis Walker
January 1990

Introduction

In the early 1990's, following the oil crisis, British Airways had to close down a number of routes and underwent massive staff redeployment and redundancy. It was sustaining huge losses, morale among staff was very low and there was widespread customer dissatisfaction.

As we enter the 1990's, British Airways is a dynamic international organization with a strong reputation. From a low of a £69.9M loss in 1981 profits have now reached in excess of £250M. It can boast a highly competent and enthusiastic workforce and a loyal following of private and business customers. It is a leader in quality and innovation.

This revival has been brought about to a large extent by an absolute determination on the part of BA's management to improve customer service to the point where it was noticeably superior to that offered by any other airline.

When Colin Marshall took over as Chief Executive of British Airways in 1983, he saw that the only possible way forward was to make the requirements of the customer pre-eminent in all aspects of the operation. 'Putting the customer first' became the theme and the rallying call of a campaign which was to last several years and was to produce a culture change which affected all its staff, its customers and its competitors.

My own role in this campaign was:

- To design the strategy underpinning the Customer First campaign and to generate senior management commitment
- Overseeing the design and implementation of all activities within the Customer First framework
- To run the Steering Group and participate in all the local management workshops
- To manage the Customer Services Department responsible for setting standards and quality assurance, training for front-line ground staff and the Customer Relations activity
- Working with Advertising and Promotions to ensure internal programmes were integrated with the Supercare campaign

- Monitoring outcomes and providing regular reviews to the Executive team.

The chief components of BA's success were:

- Establishing base research on customer needs and performance, and regularly obtaining fresh research
- Setting a clear common purpose
- Using customer data to set service standards
- Offering all staff awareness programmes at regular intervals
- Setting up and maintaining teams and tapping potential at all levels of the organization
- Investing in substantial corporate management training programmes and linking these to performance appraisal and performance pay
- Using service improvement as a marketing tool
- Keeping service innovations and initiatives within a coherent strategic framework.

Part III of this book contains a detailed account of what took place. It starts by outlining the economic and business facts which confronted BA management in the early 1980's and the philosophy behind the organizational changes which were to bring the airline such success.

Chapter 19 describes the first two years of the Customer First campaign – the training and awareness programmes, the management workshops, the internal promotion of the 'putting people first' message, and the reviews of progress in improving the service.

Chapter 20 covers the next phase of the campaign which launched three management change initiatives and which lasted until 1986. Research carried out at this stage showed that the improvements in service offered by BA had been widely recognized by customers, and that expectations of quality had been raised too. Chapter 21 describes the ways in which BA managed to consolidate its position at a time when impending privatization was creating uncertainty among employees, and developed customer loyalty by continuing to concentrate on the personal aspects of service.

British Airways would not claim to have carried out a faultless campaign; with hindsight, one can see how certain aspects of it could have been managed better. The account given here draws attention to those misjudgements while recognizing the pioneering and adventurous leadership which achieved such success. The change in fortunes of British Airways offers both inspiration and example to businesses of all kinds, and its experiences can provide lessons for those who wish to emulate its achievements.

Part I
The customer first concept

Introduction

The main purpose of Part I is to develop a service strategy framework which enables you to:

- Audit your current strengths and weaknesses
- Understand the range of initiatives and activities which have to be managed in order to produce a difference noticed by your customers and your staff.

The Part begins, however, by discussing a more fundamental question – 'What is service?'. It goes on to describe the problems of quality in service terms being personal and emotional rather than technical, making it difficult to measure and to replicate. Yet customers make judgements on the strength of whether they enjoy doing business with you. They then exercise choices. The 'anecdotes' serve as a reminder of just how much poor service is tolerated. On the other hand they indicate the enormous scope that exists for creating customer loyalty and competitive edge through service – by getting things right consistently in the eyes of the customer.

Competitive advantage must be based on a noticeable difference which meets identified customer needs better than others. This can only happen if service is treated as a strategic issue and mechanisms are put in place to make service a key organizational value.

The service strategy model starts by describing the data you need to define a strategic repositioning – data about your customers, data on the competitive context within which you are operating. It also illustrates the need for the organization's leadership to be visionary about how customer responsiveness would look from the point of view of all stakeholders.

Assuming data has been obtained and visionary thinking carried out, the model goes on to describe the many areas a service strategy affects. It demonstrates why a service strategy and a total quality programme, though they start at different ends of the spectrum, serve the same purpose. Service involves material aspects such as product reliability, delivery accuracy, as well as the personal element represented by the interaction of front-line staff with customers. Both material and personal aspects of service provide opportunities to win and lose customers, and the service strategy has to be designed to achieve excellence in both areas. The customer constantly audits your service in both areas and you must do the same.

The model serves as a template for auditing your service – finding out what you already know and what you need to know to reposition your approach to customers. It will also enable you to audit your service strengths and weaknesses systematically. In doing this work, many questions are raised about how you are organized. Are you organized in a way which produces apparent internal efficiencies, but makes it difficult to respond quickly to changing customer need? Does the organizational culture – 'the way we do things around here' – tend to support customer service or inhibit it?

Early in the Part you will be asked to complete a service 'health check' which should encourage you to read on to the more detailed suggestions for audit in this and the following Parts. Finally, analysis of just a few service incidents shows how much you can learn by listening to your customers – especially when they are complaining about your performance.

1
What is service?

I have asked this question of people from service organizations on courses and seminars many times and received many different answers, all valid in their own way because service is something very subjective and difficult to define. When buying a tangible product, there is frequently an intangible experience which may have the greater effect. Customers react differently to what appears to be the same service. The same customer can indeed react differently to the same service in different circumstances. The business executive flying out to make a difficult but important deal is not the same customer as the one returning home that night with a lucrative contract safely in his pocket. This represents the difficulty – and the challenge – for service providers and their organizations. Mood, culture and timing, as well as the customer's previous experience all affect the way service is perceived.

This concept is one that many business people are uncomfortable with, since it demands flexibility in the use of resources, giving discretion to staff who deal with customers and not relying on productivity-oriented routines. It means treating customers as individuals and setting up organizational systems which support, not hinder, this aim.

Service reputation is all about what it is like doing business with you. Is it a pleasant, rewarding experience, or one your customers would rather not repeat? Is that little bit extra being done without asking, or is getting good service like going through an army assault course?

That service standards generally need to be raised is undeniable. We all have daily experience of being a customer – buying a newspaper, getting a carpet fitted, having a haircut, eating in the canteen and so on. In each situation we make a judgement about the service. We also decide whether or not to continue to do business with the service provider. If we are not pleased we sometimes complain but usually we just decide to go somewhere else next time.

As a first step towards getting service staff or managers to discover ways of improving their own service, I ask them to write down one example of good service and one example of bad service they themselves have received. Collecting these on flip-charts provides a powerful insight into how their customers might be reacting to their service. Here are some of their examples of bad service which most people will find familiar:

- The company which will only indicate morning or afternoon for an appointment and even then doesn't keep to what has been agreed
- The company which passes you from department to department on the telephone with nobody quite able to help you
- The electrical retailer who refuses to replace one-week-old goods which have malfunctioned, saying company policy is to get them repaired
- The restaurant where the waitress refuses to serve you because 'it is not my table'
- The clinic where you find a number of other people have also got the 'first' 09.00 appointment
- The insurance company which fails to send you the form you requested, then loses your documents and refuses to pay out the claim
- The car salesman who pressurizes you and makes you feel inferior about your lack of knowledge about cars
- The aircraft cabin crew who find it more enjoyable to talk among themselves than to service their passengers
- The shop assistant who always has to ask someone else the answer to your query.

Most people doing this exercise find it easier to remember bad experiences than good ones. Later in the book we'll look again at these examples and see how they can be avoided.

2

Service strategy

'Putting the customer first' is an admirable intention, but it will only be more than that if there is a proper service strategy. The two main objectives of this strategy are to create a difference which is observable or measurable by the customers and to have real impact on the way things are done inside the company.

The service strategy is a central part of a company's business strategy which will also cover profit objectives, markets, technology and so on. It is central because it defines the company's internal culture as well as its desired external image. It needs to be put in writing and communicated widely, so that no one is in any doubt about what it is designed to achieve. It needs to be matched by an organization structure designed for customer response. It must include:

- Customers' needs and expectations. No company can survive if its customers' needs are either not fully defined or ignored when known. In most service industries customers have different options; British Caledonian's slogan, 'We never forget you've got a choice', illustrated their awareness of this fact.
- Competitors' activities. Without knowledge of what your main competitors are doing, it is impossible to set out to gain advantage through the quality and innovation of your services. You should at least be familiar with the visible results of competitors' strategies. You need to know why customers are using their products and services rather than your own.

Both of these areas need to be subjected to regular audit and assessment which in itself should be part of your service strategy (See Chapters 3 and 4 for detailed ideas on how to do this.)

- Vision of the future. Listening to customers and watching the competition are obviously important processes, but they may not be sufficient to sustain differentiation and customer satisfaction over the longer term. The companies that stand apart from the rest have visionary leaders who encourage experimentation and change and enable people to create a vision of the future. This is not a projection of the future on the basis of present position, but a clear picture of where you would like to be and how to get there.

Let us now look at what customers receive or, at least, expect to receive for their money. It is usually a combination of material service and personal service. If you are buying a toaster, the material aspects will be most important; if you are staying in a hotel, the personal aspects of service may be the uppermost. But in each case you hope that both material and personal service will be excellent. This is an important consideration when developing a strategy for service: it has to ensure that the customer is consistently well served in both ways.

Material service

The *product* itself has to be reliable and do what it is specified to do.

The *environment* must reflect the quality of the organization – shoddy premises invariably raise questions about other aspects of a company's standards and performance.

The *delivery systems* must work; this includes distribution, scheduling, accountancy and computerized paperwork, job organization and so on – it does not matter how good a product is, if it arrives late or damaged, if it is not to the customer's specification, or if the order and account paperwork do not match.

All these points must be covered by the service strategy.

Personal service

How good a company is to deal with usually depends on the people it employs. Their *knowledge* and *skills* are crucial to the company's ability to fulfil the expectations expressed in the service strategy. Staff who have direct contact with customers have the greatest effect on the company's reputation, but those behind the scenes must not be ignored as they service those who are dealing with the customers, as well as creating the products and many of the delivery systems.

The *attitude* of staff towards the customers can also strongly support or badly undermine a company's service strategy. If they do not believe in, and demonstrate commitment to, the customer, then the service will not match the image being promoted. It is important, therefore, to know where they stand (using a carefully constructed attitude survey).

The *people systems* must be designed to motivate staff to support the service strategy. Selection criteria should reflect the need for customer focus, induction should introduce it at an early stage, 'technical' training should reinforce and not conflict, and performance appraisal should develop objectives relating to service performance and influence reward accordingly. The way people are organized and the way they are managed must also be compatible with giving good service.

Clearly, any organization determined to become more customer-oriented needs to examine its performance in each of the above areas. Later chapters show how to carry out an audit of 'organizational health' prior to, or as part of, a service improvement programme. The activity of auditing should then become a natural part of the continuous improvement process.

Try the following brief health check for your own organization. If you can honestly say 'yes' to all the questions, then you probably don't need to read the rest of the book. Although, remember, no service situation stands still!

Service health check

- Do you know your customers and are you clear about their needs?
- Have you communicated these needs to your staff?
- Have clear service standards been set and communicated?
- Are you sure about how service can give you an edge over your competitors?
- Have you clearly defined the skills and knowledge required by your staff to deliver quality service?
- Have the skills of managing your service business been identified and programmes set up to give all managers these skills?
- Do you know how much poor quality is costing you and what the main causes of poor quality are?
- Do you have a customer complaints system?
- Do you have a corporate mission?
- Has this mission been communicated to your staff and set in the context of their work?
- Do systems exist which assure you of quality products or services?
- Do your selection procedures reflect a quality company?

Service strategy model

The concept of the service strategy can be presented in the form of a model (Figure 2.1). It can be used in auditing organizational health and in devising service quality improvement programmes, as will be seen later on.

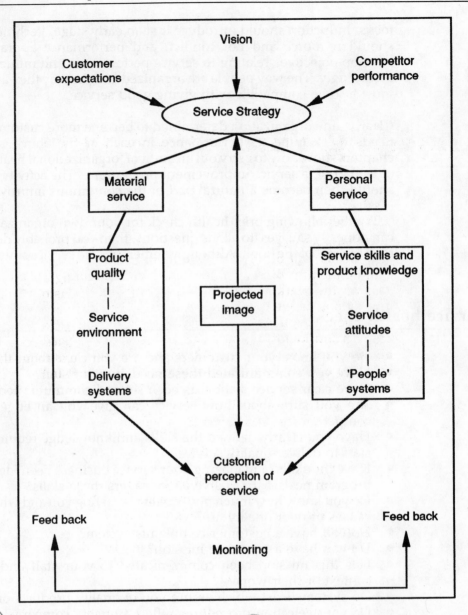

Figure 2.1 Service strategy model

3

Knowing your customers

Customers' service needs change as do their expectations of how well these needs will be met. Research, therefore, can never give a totally accurate picture. But it is important before planning a strategic shift to focus on the marketplace, to take a snapshot of customers' needs and expectations as well as their perceptions of your current performance. Subsequently, you need to be able to check from time to time to gauge your progress and identify trends and changes taking place.

Before carrying out a piece of market research, it is important to audit what you already know about your customers. For instance:

- Analyse your complaints (and compliments): what are your customers saying about your current performance; are they giving hints as to what their real expectations are?
- Are there any industry data about customer needs and industry performance? how do you rate?
- Ask your staff how satisfied they think your customers are. It is easy for managers to ignore how much staff know from day-to-day contact with customers, and mechanisms to collect such data are invariably lacking.
- If staff and their families are customers of their own services, there may be a further valuable source of data to compare with "real" customer data.

Relying on unsolicited customer comment is rarely sufficient to give a good picture of customer views. It is in every service organization's interest to elicit as much customer comment as possible. Few companies have a systematic way of doing this. A comment card left in a hotel bedroom may generate extra feedback, but it is no substitute for face-to-face contact.

The service strategy must include a means of seeking reactions and it must express clearly the company's attitude towards customer complaints. 'Satisfaction or your money back' is a bold promise to customers, designed to give a competitive edge in the marketplace. Such a promise must be backed up by clear guidelines to customer contact staff within the organization. Service staff need to know what they are empowered to do to satisfy customers' needs and, particularly, to rescue dissatisfied customers.

One of the initial tasks of any piece of research, is to establish who the real customers are; this may not simply be the actual consumer of the product or service. In the case of an airline passenger, for instance, the secretary, company travel manager, spouse or even hotel porter may be more important in terms of the decision about which airline to use. Knowledge of the real decision makers and their needs must, therefore, play a part in your service strategy. In a complex manufacturing chain, where your company plays just one part, you need to establish the key points in the chain – the people who change or influence the buying pattern most: they are your prime customers. If you believe you don't know enough about your customers, then it is worth your while taking a snapshot of customer opinion and need. This may mean doing research which you can repeat at regular intervals to compare findings, or it may mean developing a platform for progressive and perhaps more focused research in the future. This depends largely on how dynamic you judge your marketplace to be. The more dynamic, the less useful regular repeat surveys are and the greater the need for a flexible approach. Survey data also indicate the customers whom you should target to develop business partnerships – where business growth becomes a common objective.

It is beyond the scope of this book to discuss market research in detail. However, the following are some options you might like to explore:

- Do you want the research to be obviously about your own company, its image, its performance; or are you more interested in industry pointers? The research could be neutral (What do customers want or expect from a car dealership?) or partisan (How satisfied were you with the after-sales service at Bloggs Motors?). The two approaches can be combined in some settings by asking general industry questions first, followed by ones about your own company. (See Chapter 19 for an example of the latter approach.)
- If you are not sure of the language your customers use to describe your business, you may need to do a qualitative piece of research first (again, at industry or company level as appropriate). This is best carried out by one or more group discussions led by a researcher, or through a small number of in-depth interviews. The research itself gives useful pointers to the key issues perceived by your customers, in addition to providing the language which you can then use to generate a larger-scale quantitative piece of research.
- Given the earlier comments about material and personal aspects of service, with the latter often dominating customer perception, it is important that research covers both. The tendency in the past has been to concentrate on product-related research, but not to analyse how the

customer feels about doing business with you. Questions about warmth and friendliness, accessibility by telephone, prompt response, use of name, treating you as an individual and being thanked for your business are at least as important as preferred colour and other such product specifications.

- Most large-scale research will be carried out by interview or questionnaire, and possibly by a combination of the two. The presence of an interviewer means there is a possibility to probe and gain more depth, but it is more time consuming, more difficult to analyse and, consequently, more expensive. On the other hand, a questionnaire is difficult to design well and may have a poor response rate. Professional advice should be sought to design an approach specific to your company and its marketplace and probably to carry out the research and report the findings. The independence of the research company often gives the research more credibility inside the company.

  Focus groups and telephone interviewing are two other related methods of gaining the views of customers in your marketplace; each has its pros and cons.

- Choice of method will also depend on how you intend to carry out future surveys. Questionnaires are easy to repeat and compare. Interviews allow you to ask comparative questions, but also to progress to new areas relatively easy.

- Once you have taken the initial snapshot, the research will indicate where effort should be focused to improve performance and meet customer needs. It is these critical areas that require monitoring most. Some options for doing this are mini snapshots (of those issues), mystery shopper exercises to test real performance, comment cards to elicit customer reactions. This is particularly important when you are concerned with image, reputation and so on.

- Research in itself achieves little unless there is an effective means of feeding back the data to those in the organization who can do something about it, and unless corrective action can be taken. Data must be presented in such a way as to command attention and result in action. It should also be appropriate to its audience and lead naturally to setting up challenging but achievable targets for improvement.

  Because little attention is paid to these aspects, much research and performance data remain unread. A mechanism which enables service managers and providers to note and discuss data needs to be established. Simply sending out a monthly report or a memo to do better in the weaker areas is unlikely to result in change. The data provide a real opportunity for staff to become involved in improving services and monitoring the effect. This leads to a sense of collective responsibility for service performance.

- Research aims to elicit customer views in important areas. It should be complemented by what the customer tells you in the form of complaints, compliments and suggestions.

Whilst this last sample is small, these customers have taken the trouble to make contact – you should take notice of them.

Your company needs to consider its stance towards complaints in particular. Word processing allows these to be handled efficiently through standard letters, but is this what the customer wants? Most research suggests that individual treatment is the best way to respond, but your organization and resources have to be geared up to handle this sensitively and knowledgeably. You should have a policy on: style of response; approach to compensation and follow-up action. You should also have a means of analysing complaints so that the learning opportunities are used to the full. (See Chapter 17 for more detail on handling complaints.) The service company which shuns its complaining customers is taking a very short-term view, as the following model illustrates:

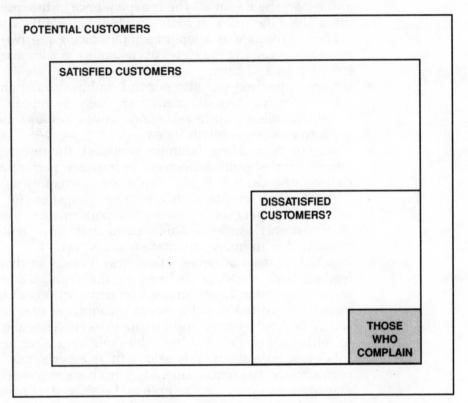

Figure 3.1 Complaining customers as a proportion of the potential market

Of all dissatisfied customers only around 5 per cent actually make a complaint. Of those complaints, many can be answered satisfactorily by a clarification of the situation. Most of the rest can be answered through negotiation. Only a few of the customers who complain cannot be re-established as supporters of your product or service. All the rest offer an opportunity to correct and learn. Doing it well can actually enhance your service reputation. Future business depends on reputation, which is created by both satisfied and dissatisfied customers talking to friends and colleagues; and we know that we tell our bad experiences to more than twice the number of people we tell our good experiences to. Dissatisfied customers can, therefore, do immeasurable damage to a business.

4

Knowing your competitors

Being better than the competition rarely means doing one thing vastly better. It usually means doing many little things just that little bit better. It is important, therefore, to know what your competitors are doing. Industry research will not necessarily provide a detailed analysis, but it will indicate what criteria are most important to customers. It makes sense to put your efforts into monitoring your competitors' performance in these areas.

Before doing this, there is a more fundamental question which needs to be addressed: 'Who are your competitors?' In many cases the answer is obvious; but it is very easy to make faulty assumptions. For instance, car dealers traditionally saw other dealerships selling different makes as their prime competitors. However, there have recently been some surprising new entrants to the marketplace who have steadily taken away business – often very profitable business – from all car dealers: Kwikfit and Standard Motorist Centres are supplying batteries, exhausts and tyres, whilst similar organizations are now moving into full servicing. Halfords now have a multi-million pound business in car parts, and supermarkets such as ASDA and Sainsbury's are looking to use their retail experience to gain a part of a business worth £20 billion in the UK. Brewers can no longer view other brewers as the sole competition; they are up against the whole of the leisure industry competing for customers' time and money. As Figure 2.1 showed, we cannot devise a service strategy if we don't have a feel for the competitive environment in which we operate.

Customer research, therefore, needs to compare performance on aspects such as value for money, reliability, courtesy and environment across a range of service providers with whom the customer does business. The real competitor is the company judged to offer the best. Figure 4.1 shows how accuracy of delivery to a retailer is assessed by the retailer. Your strongest competitors may not be in the same business as yourself, but they are influencing your customers' expectations.

The type of analysis in Figure 4.1 could be repeated across a whole range of service dimensions and provides a picture of strengths and weaknesses against your obvious, and not so obvious, competitors. For instance, in

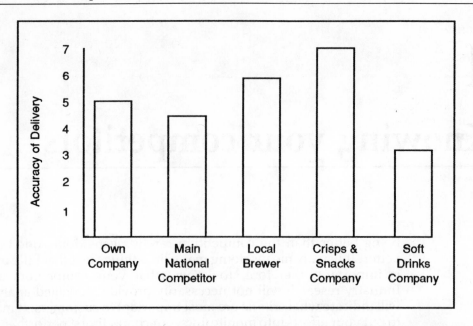

Figure 4.1   Accuracy of delivery by various companies assessed by a retailer

Figure 4.2 a supermarket is compared with its competitors on a number of dimensions.

Some entries in the matrix will be Yes/No, others will comprise specific facts. In some areas you will need to add a qualitative judgement to assess who has the competitive edge. You will see the information mixes material and personal service factors. It shows where competitors are much the same; it shows where differentiation occurs. If one competitor differs from the rest in one respect, this shows where innovation is taking place (or where outdated practices still remain).

From this and other data it is possible to make a guess at your competitors' service strategy and make plans to counteract it where necessary. Use your competitors' service as a customer – find out how it feels to do business with them. What areas are better? How could you match or better them? For many years, managers in British Airways were discouraged from using rival airlines, except perhaps where the two airlines operated a pooling or cartel arrangement. A more competitive airline world meant it was essential to find out what competitors such as Cathay Pacific, Virgin Atlantic, People's Express and Air New Zealand were doing. In-depth studies of competitors, looking at all aspects of their service mix, were included in the monthly service performance results and discussed at senior team meetings; this was a sure way of avoiding complacency.

Developing customer partnerships to keep customers loyal not only makes sound economic sense, it also keeps the competition out by ensuring you are closer to understanding and meeting customer's needs

Organization Service Factor	You	Competitor 1	Competitor 2	Competitor 3
Self service				
No. of check-outs				
No. of front-line staff				
Packers				
Car Parking spaces				
Aisle width				
Loyalty scheme				
Quality of staff				
Electronic P.O.S (point of sale)				
Children's facilities				
Customer product videos				

Figure 4.2   Comparison of supermarkets by service criteria

than your competitors ever can be. Ignoring the competition, however, is a foolish thing to do since they have customers who are currently choosing not to do business with you. If you don't know why, then you have little chance of converting them to use your services instead.

So, first know your competitors; then analyse what they are doing differently and better and the effect it is having on the marketplace. Market share data, when available, will indicate this and you will need to support this by your own intelligence gathering activities – obtaining brochures, trying products yourself, asking your customers and so on.

Systematic collation of the data is important so that you can assess where your relative strengths and weaknesses are.

5

Developing a vision

Once you have carried out the customer research exercises and analysed the competition you are in a position to think of the future. Where do you want to take your company and what type of company would you like it to be? You may already have a five-year plan in which certain business goals are set out, but are these simply the result of projecting from the current situation or do they reflect a vision of the future? Developing a 'mission statement' is an integral part of preparing a service strategy. It should clearly indicate the nature, content and purpose of the initiatives required to bring about an improvement in service performance. Excellence is not achieved by accident: it occurs as a result of having a clear vision of success.

Visioning should initially be the work of the senior team. They need to produce a statement of the values by which the company wishes to operate. Many managers, being constrained by tradition and their own experience, find this a difficult exercise. They are happier projecting on the basis of known facts than dealing with discontinuity, adventure or risk. But these are the elements which ultimately lead to real culture change. Having the key values which the organization aspires to fully communicated and understood leads to clearly focused objectives and target setting systems; people are appraised and rewarded according to these values.

Although the senior managers ideally develop the corporate vision, departments can be asked to develop their own mission statements to support the corporate statements.

Chapter 12 has an outline programme for taking the senior team through a visioning exercise, setting out values in the context of a mission statement and agreeing the action required to get it widely accepted within the organization. Visions which are shared by senior teams will not happen by accident. Time has to be allocated and, of course, there are always other priorities – like running today's business rather than worrying about tomorrow's.

One of the best ways to initiate debate on a vision of the future is to use the customer data to show there is a need for a repositioning. If there is still doubt, establish an internal survey and use this data as well (see

Chapter 12). These data will show the need for a common purpose or cause, for new approaches in dealing with customers and staff. The data stimulates discussion which can then be directed towards the question 'What could it be like?'.

Ron Zemke, co-author of *Service America*, had this to say about vision:

Visionary leaders have always struggled to put their images and ideas into words. Written words. It is an act of creation and communication. The great manifestos shape and focus history. Indeed, they are history. The Magna Carta, the Declaration of Independence, the Preamble to the US Constitution – and, for that matter, Mein Kampf and Das Kapital – come to mind as documents that not only communicated ideas, but brought dramatic changes into being.

The power of the written word to set direction, communicate purpose and guide action, is understood by leaders in many venues. Heads of universities, associations, trade unions, charities, businesses, commissions, bodies and boards of all sorts, struggle regularly to clarify and communicate their visions of their organizations' proper missions and methods.

Out of a vision exercise can come written mission statements – an important first step in the strategic planning process and fundamental to a unit's existence. An effective mission statement can help to satisfy people's needs to be involved in something worthwhile, to beat the opposition and to earn respect. It is thus a general declaration of attitude and philosophy which could cover broad organizational concerns such as:

- Marketplace and customers
- Products and service
- Geography and technology
- Survival, growth and profitability
- Self concept and desired public image.

Two examples of mission statements are shown below: that of a district health service and a manufacturing organization. British Airways' mission appears in Chapter 19.

These two organizations have taken different approaches to describing and communicating the visions of their senior teams. If explained well and debated thoroughly, a mission statement can permeate the entire organization. If treated purely as an exercise in creative writing, it will be worthless and, worse, may be ridiculed by the very people at whom it is aimed. A company which is really confident in its mission statement can use it as a marketing tool – challenging customers, competitors and the community to judge it by its own stated values. The statement can become a customer charter and provide a real competitive edge.

PEMBROKESHIRE
HEALTH AUTHORITY

ASPIRING TO EXCELLENCE

To serve the people in Pembrokeshire
to the highest professional
and technical standards

To promote healthy lifestyles amongst
our community

To respond quickly and sensitively
to changing health care needs

To be efficient and imaginative
in operating, managing
and marketing our services

To create a satisfying work
environment in which staff can
realize their full potential

ICI FIBRES

OUR MISSION

WE MUST ACHIEVE EXCELLENCE
IN EVERYTHING WE DO FROM
RESEARCH, THROUGH MANUFACTURING
AND SELLING TO FINAL DELIVERY
TO THE CUSTOMER

EXCELLENCE IS THE KEY TO
COMPETITIVE EDGE AND A BETTER
QUALITY OF LIFE FOR ALL

WE WILL SUCCEED ONLY BY
DELIVERING THE PROMISE EACH
AND EVERY TIME

6
Organizing for service

The organization which has decided on a Customer First strategy must be designed to support such a culture shift.

Given the emphasis on productivity in the past decade, it is not surprising that many organizations are structured primarily for efficiency. Service quality cuts across functional barriers, so a re-think on resources is necessary. The danger otherwise is that the service strategy will be doomed because of self-protection, wrong priorities and basic lack of understanding. A strong production or finance orientation will make it difficult for the organization to focus totally on the customer. If meeting output targets or coming in on budget are allowed priority over service to the customer, the service strategy will fail. If decisions are always made on the basis of resource efficiency rather than customer need, then staff and customers will see that customer service is not the prime value – whatever mission statement and training programmes say.

A useful way of testing how customer-oriented an organization is, is to look at management objectives – how many reflect cost, efficiency, product output and how many reflect quality and customer service? If focusing on the customer is a way of life these will have at least equal billing. The following are points by which to audit or design customer orientation in an organization:

1. Is the organization structure related to the structure of the marketplace?

- Are market segmentation and customer types reflected in the internal business definitions, marketing department structure and even the production structures?
- Do the different market segments/customer types have different product and service mixes and service packages? Does the organization add differential value to these segments and how is this reflected in technical service, training support, packaging, etc?
- Do customer partnership decisions produce real differences in organizational priorities and structure – for example, in technology and system developments, promotional support, accounting?

- Is customer geography/demography reflected in the sales, distribution and customer service structures?
- Is technical support provided on the basis of customer need or as a conglomerate business support unit?

2. How responsive is the organization to shifts in the marketplace?

- How quickly can the organization adapt to changing customer mix and needs?
- Can the organization cope with remoting by technology some aspects of the service package to customers' premises?
- How speedily can new products and service innovations be brought to the marketplace; are competitors known to be able to do it faster?
- Is there a market research function and is its role given prominence in the organization?

3. Does organizational culture incorporate the following:

- Honesty and openness
- Flexibility
- An environment where full potential can be reached
- Desire to listen to customers and staff?

Or is the culture:

- Hierarchical
- Procedural
- Slow to respond
- Based on experience rather than risk taking?

4. Are the roles of managers:

- Defined in terms of managing the service experience
- Based on clarity of vision
- Established as enablers and coaches
- Designed for availability – to staff and customers?

Or are they:

- Defined in terms of budget
- Set up as inspectors and inhibitors
- Desk-bound and meetings-oriented?

5. Culture can be viewed from a number of perspectives both externally and internally. It is useful to look at an organization's culture from the point of view of its managers, compared with that of its customers and staff (Figure 6.1).

If an organization is to be changed to be more customer oriented, the customers' perception must be understood, and the attitudes of staff must be known. The model demonstrates that if a real difference is to be made, a 'manager knows best' attitude is not acceptable.

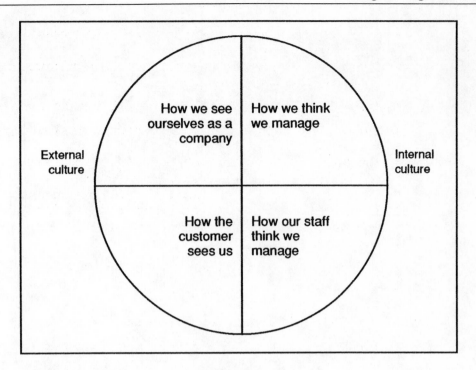

Figure 6.1   Different views of an organization's culture

If cultural norms at management level do not support the new emphasis and style, then a major programme of education is required. Managers who are unable to accept these new structures or values are not going to bring about the change required, and will undermine all the plans. Commitment by managers is a prerequisite for success.

Organizational structural change where identified as necessary has to be handled at the start – creating an opportunity to test the new philosophy of the organization, handling exiting in a way which preserves dignity and self esteem.

7
Auditing material service

It is now time to take a long hard look at your service strengths and weaknesses. This chapter concentrates on reviewing material aspects of service, which is perhaps the easiest part of service to audit. However, managers are not always the best judges of what is important and this chapter, therefore, describes an approach to increasing the level of honesty and objectivity of the audit.

Two examples will suffice to explain why managers' perspectives are not always helpful. In the early days of the British Airways Putting People First programme (described in detail in Part III) senior managers took part in an exercise designed to show that personal service outranks material service when customers choose an airline. People were asked to rate a number of factors according to whether they produced – a positive feeling, a neutral feeling or a negative feeling. So, for instance, most people would rate 'a warm welcome' as producing a positive feeling.

When the managers did this exercise, the results indicated that material aspects of the service were more important than personal aspects. One interesting response was on the subject of 'clean toilets'. Most managers had ticked the positive feelings box. Most customers, however, indicated neutrality to this factor, which surprised the managers. Managers appreciate the problems of maintaining clean toilets; customers, on the other hand, take them for granted and only react when they are not clean. So managers don't always see things naturally from the customer viewpoint.

Another example of this concerns a survey of private medicine expectations, where patients were asked to rank aspects of service in priority order. Senior medical staff were asked to do the same exercise and produced almost the reverse response. Material aspects were at the top of their lists, while the patients' lists were dominated by personal aspects. Again, patients were shown to take many of the technical aspects of medical care for granted. The medical staff were rightly proud of their technical achievements; the patients wanted the personal touch.

Clearly, both perspectives are valid, but it is important that the audit is strongly influenced by customer needs, not managerial satisfaction.

As we said in Chapter 2, material service can usefully be subdivided into the three headings as follows:

- Product
- Environment
- Delivery system

and each should be subjected to the audit. The market research already discussed, and any unsolicited customer comments and complaints, should all be included in the audit.

Product

We are concerned here with quality of product, rather than pricing policy, selling and marketing which are other important aspects of customer satisfaction. It is evident that in many situations customers are prepared to pay more for reliable, quality products and services.

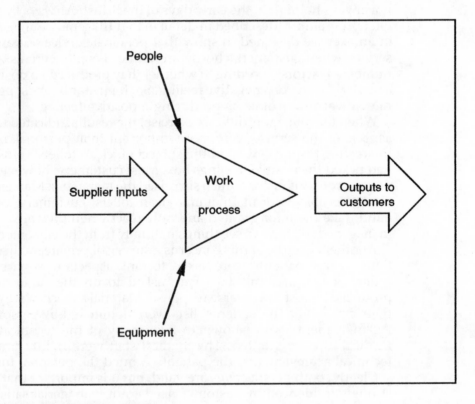

Figure 7.1   The production process

The way products are advertised and promoted is, of course, important since this contributes strongly to customer expectations. Failure to satisfy these expectations becomes a problem. In 1983, British Airways took a conscious decision to stop advertising about service, since it was not delivering the standards implied by claims such as 'We take more care of you'. In 1985 British Rail's 'We're getting there' campaign became a hostage to fortune when services failed. (Service performance as a competitive marketing tool is discussed in Chapter 16.)

To assess whether a product has quality, you must ask: Does it do what it is supposed to do to a very high level of reliability and how does it compare with its competitors? Every business has a product:

Restaurants	have food and drink
Hotels	have rooms, beds, bathrooms, a restaurant, and leisure facilities
Airlines	have aircraft seats, food, films, airport facilities
Shops	have goods on sale
Manufacturers	have goods produced.

In each case the aim must be for high quality production on a regular and consistent basis. This is done through chains of business processes which take a number of inputs and produce a number of outputs. Figure 7.1 shows one of these processes – the suppliers and customers can be external or internal.

The outputs are what is provided to customers and the inputs are what we gain from our suppliers in the way of raw materials. The process is the way we use equipment and people operating to specified standards and procedures which should be determined by customer requirement. If we find we are not producing what our customers want, then one of the following must be happening:

- The specification is not clear
- Equipment or facilities are not right for the job
- Staff don't have the knowledge or skills to produce the specification
- Standards for measuring how well the process is doing do not exist or have not been communicated to those carrying out the process.

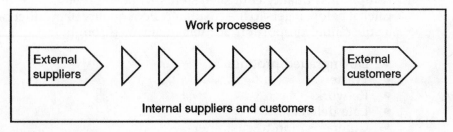

Figure 7.2   Work processes

In any organization there are many processes which have to work together to provide an integrated service to the customer (Figure 7.2). At one end of the chain are the customers who pay the wages – although they may also be part of a complex production, distribution and sales chain. At the other end are the suppliers of raw materials. In between are the internal customers who need to be served. This means that the service strategy has to reach internal servicing departments such as personnel, management services, stores and engineering. These staff must be included in your programme of initiatives, if they are not to feel second-class and undermine your efforts. The chain will break at its weakest point, resulting in poor quality at the customer interface.

The process of quality improvement requires the whole organization to be involved. Management must ensure that:

- Tasks are clearly specified
- Performance data are communicated to those carrying out the tasks
- The means of regulating the processes of work are available to those doing the work.

If management fails to do this, the sole responsibility for poor quality is theirs. Once these systems are in place, quality becomes a collective responsibility.

If your audit shows a number of weak areas, priorities have to be decided on the basis of:

- Which hits the customer hardest?
- How much would it cost to put right?
- How long will it take to put right?

Quality has to be attended to issue by issue – there are no short cuts, therefore priorities have to be set and a plan formulated to progressively improve quality. One-off solutions should not be sought. Quality improvement should become an ongoing natural part of the work process. One way of involving the staff is to set up corrective action teams or other forms of task teams (see Chapter 15).

Too many organizations institutionalize poor quality. They set up complicated quality control systems – not to prevent poor quality but to catch it before it gets to the customer. Poor quality of product can cost them a substantial proportion of their turnover through:

- Downgraded product
- Waste
- Re-work
- Late delivery
- Compensation to customers
- Quality inspectors

- Complaints department
- Machine downtime.

Producing good quality also costs money, but it is substantially less than the cost of poor quality. The answer is to seek the root cause of the problems and install real and lasting solutions.

Various structured approaches to quality can be found in the works of Deming, Crosby, Juran and others. However, it is possible to form your own commonsense approach to quality and involve your workforce in the diagnosis, corrective action and implementation of solutions in a process of continuous improvement. (Some guidelines are given in Chapter 13.)

Many organizations are deciding to set up a more structured process of quality assurance and are seeking certification of their procedures through standards such as the British Standards Institution's BS5750 or the equivalent international standard ISO9000 series. International companies such as Ford with its Q101 programme are developing their own quality standards which they impose on their suppliers. This trend applies predominantly to manufacturing processes, but other areas such as distribution, purchasing and engineering are recognizing the potential. Chemical companies such as ICI are seeking ways of using this kind of procedure for continuous process chemical production; they recognize the competitive edge it could provide in their global markets. The Single European Market of 1992 provides further opportunities for common standards to be of benefit to Europe-wide customers.

As well as commercial benefits, quality assurance with its continuous audit process built in, has value in terms of improving work definition, management processes and practice. It can also help to avoid cutting corners, inconsistencies and so on. However, having procedures which can be audited does not guarantee that these are the best procedures. Continuous improvement must still be the aim of a broader, total quality programme. Quality assurance becomes a natural and integral part of such a programme, providing a continual source of corrective action.

Environment

The environment is not as tangible as the product, but it certainly plays a large part in the customer's decision whether or not to do business with you. 'The food isn't that good, but the surroundings are convivial' is often said by way of recommendation. Your objective review must attempt to define and understand the impact of your service environment. Environment is obviously important to restaurants, shops, cinemas, hotels, airlines, banks, car dealerships, libraries and so on. But it is of concern to manufacturing companies too. What is the reception foyer like? What image of the company does it portray? What showroom facilities exist? Do you get offered a cup of coffee? What is the loading bay like? All these are part of the environment in which you do business with your customer.

'There is something about that place that makes me feel uncomfortable.' The following is a list of things you might look at:

- Quality of furniture/furnishings
- Colour combinations
- Lighting
- Space available for customers
- Queueing systems
- Barriers between customers and you, and your staff and products
- Signage and promotional materials
- Cleanliness and tidiness
- Amount of privacy
- Customer facilities such as coffee and phones
- Ease of finding the way around
- Car parking facilities
- Ease of accessing products and services.

All of these affect the image of an organization. Customers walking into an untidy foyer are bound to wonder about the state of your production or management and so on. The damage done to your image will far exceed the cost of keeping the place tidy.

Aspects of the environment which affect staff must also be looked at. This includes facilities, procedures and work organization. If the comfort of staff as well as customers is not taken account of, they and the service they give deteriorates. One example of a problem area is security screens; they are obviously important in banks and railway stations, but some are so badly positioned, you get neck and backache using them. Staff will have a wealth of information and ideas on aspects like this and should never be ignored. Again, managers do not always know best.

Improving the environment is often relatively simple: installing a coffee machine, moving the reception desk, brightening the place up with some plants and so on can be easy and cheap. It is a good idea for staff to work on improvements through task teams. Customer perceptions of improvements are difficult to measure, but the investment of time and effort is definitely worthwhile.

Delivery systems

We are talking here about packaging, warehousing and distribution, transport, customer information, ordering and billing systems, all of which need to be oriented towards the customer. Far too often they are complex, and are dictated by internal operational or production demands and care little for the needs of the customer. Some examples of delivery systems going wrong are:

- Food cold when served at the table
- Baggage in Hong Kong whilst you are in New York
- An early morning call booked but not made
- The company promising to deliver on Wednesday but arriving on Thursday saying the load scheduled had been too big for the van
- Travel agents closing on a Saturday afternoon to avoid the need for extra staff
- Goods damaged in transit ('Well we did put a fragile label on it!')
- Late arrival of your commuter train
- Having to accept a different colour car from the one you ordered (unless you are prepared to wait another six weeks)
- Receiving a credit card statement for something you didn't buy
- Getting a nasty final reminder ten days after you paid the bill
- Looking in horror at your newly laid but wrong colour carpet.

Most people will have personally experienced a number of such delivery system failures and many more besides. Customers put up with a lot. But service providers who want to achieve and sustain a quality image cannot tolerate such inefficiencies.

Other delivery systems are set up on the assumption that quality won't always be right – warranties, compensation policies and replacement policies have in themselves to deliver efficiently and must be part of the audit. It is obvious that a no-arguments replacement policy such as that employed by Marks & Spencer has to work each and every time. Arguments about what a warranty does or does not cover are not conducive to further business, nor is a compensation system based on the 'assault course' principle going to win you any friends. Greater emphasis on product liability in the future will mean you have to get these areas right.

Your complaints analysis and your research will point to 'delivery' problems. These will be trickier to put right, they have to be a priority as they will consistently produce quality problems until the root cause is removed. Again, the staff who use the delivery systems are the most useful source of lasting solutions – so involve them, don't ignore them.

As well as being the cause of most customer and staff frustration, delivery systems are often the most difficult to fix. They frequently have no clear ownership as they cross a number of departmental boundaries giving, at least, shared ownership and, at worst, no ownership at all. You need to break down disciplinary barriers to solve them. However, doing this will provide the strongest signal of your seriousness to put quality into every aspect of the organization. (Chapters 11 and 13 deal with auditing your own performance and instituting a service improvement programme.)

8

Auditing personal service

Research into customer satisfaction has shown that personal aspects of service very often override material ones. Even when a product itself does not meet expectations, excellent personal service can redeem the situation.

Quality of service depends a lot on those who are providing it feeling good about themselves. Bearing in mind that image and reputation are often created or undermined by the performance of our front-line service providers, it is important that we audit personal service just as objectively and comprehensively as material service. Again analysis of customer comments and market research will provide plenty of data.

Since personal service is going to form an important part of your service strategy, you need to audit strengths and weaknesses under the headings outlined in the service strategy model:

- Skills/knowledge
- Attitudes
- People systems.

The review should be applied not only to customer contact staff, but also to other staff who are part of the team and who can contribute to or undermine your service reputation. It is also important to review management against the same criteria, since they provide a service to staff and create the climate in which good or bad service takes place.

Skills/knowledge

Lack of skill or knowledge is immediately offputting to customers. If they have no confidence in the individual dealing with them, they will lose confidence in the organization. The individual also loses self-confidence and tends to avoid opportunities to give good service, damaging the company's reputation even more. Important elements of skill and knowledge to reveiw are:

- Technical knowledge
- Product knowledge
- Knowledge about the business and the organization
- Customer handling skills such as selling, problem solving, clarifying, summarizing
- Handling complaints and aggression
- Being polite and courteous

Many of these are also important for staff behind the scenes. They may rarely meet customers, but they act as representatives of your company outside work and they do all have internal customers.

If you are trying to create a people and service environment, then all staff should understand this from induction training onwards. Training in customer awareness is dealt with in Chapter 13 and must be an integral part of your strategy for achieving and maintaining a consistent service reputation. Such skills and knowledge need to be monitored in action and this can be done by:

- Supervisory observation
- Interviewing customers after an interaction
- Peer group monitoring
- Self analysis.

To monitor effectively, clear standards of performance have to be defined and communicated as part of the training programme. Some examples of standards, monitoring and use of the data collected are illustrated in Chapter 13.

>Managerial skills and knowledge are also important since managers, by example, set modes of behaviour for their staff. A supportive environment for service needs to be cultivated. Managers need to understand and believe in the vision of the company and develop a mission for themselves and their unit to support the achievement of the vision.〈(The skills of managing a service business are covered fully in Chapter 15.) Too often managerial skills are an afterthought in any improvement programme, yet, as was shown earlier, improvement depends on management defining targets and expectations for those below them.

>Supervisors require the same skills and knowledge as their staff, with a more detailed understanding of policy and procedures to support those dealing with the customers. Supervisors who are 'guardians of the rule book' are rarely contributing to a climate of good service. A good supervisor has the skills to train and develop staff, set performance objectives, give feedback, counsel and use other 'helping' strategies. 〈

The audit of skills and knowledge within the organization should point to areas which are deficient, and plans should be drawn up at both a group and an individual level to:

- Deliver the appropriate training
- Restructure the work
- Move square pegs from round holes
- Provide policy and procedure support.

Attitudes

Staff can be well equipped with knowledge and skills, but not have the desire or the willingness to deliver good customer service. Many 'poor service' stories reflect rude or 'couldn't care less' attitudes towards the customer. Poorly motivated people can be very damaging indeed, particularly face-to-face with the customer. The attitude of a manager or supervisor influences staff attitudes to the customer and their job. It is often what they don't say rather than what they do say that exposes the 'lip service' managers. Attitudes are not easy to define but the behaviour which results from certain attitudes is often very easy to observe as is their impact on customers. This is another area where good data are required, and the best way to start is to ask the people in your organization about:

- The customer
- Their role
- The organization they work for
- Their management.

There are other useful indicators of wellbeing, such as sickness and absence rates, errors and disputes. Before launching a strategy designed to improve your service performance, it is important to know where the agents of that strategy stand. A snapshot attitude survey will help you to see the gaps between expectation and delivery and the reasons for them. A customer awareness programme can then be designed to close the gaps. (Attitude surveys are covered in more detail in Chapter 11.)

An awareness programme would need to cover:

- The vision of the organization
- Customer expectations
- Current performance levels and inhibitors
- Service standards
- Personal presentation
- Assertiveness
- Collective ownership of problems
- Positive attitudes
- The impact of body language.

Attitudes are not always easy to change, and there are likely to be some people who do not respond to the programme and improve their behaviour towards customers. You have to consider whether impact of such staff on customers and colleagues can be tolerated and, if not, do something about it. This leads us to the final section relating to personal service – people systems.

People systems

Under this heading, we include:

- Recruitment
- Selection
- Induction
- Training
- Appraisal
- Promotion
- Pay and incentives
- Uniform issue
- Policies and procedures
- Facilities and equipment.

All of these people systems have to be designed so as to support and not inhibit good service. This means a comprehensive review and, where necessary, overhaul of these systems. For instance:

- *Recruitment* 1. Do job and person profiles reflect the importance of service?
  2. Do advertisements stress the importance of service?
  3. Are your procedures applicant-oriented?

- *Selection* 1. Are your selection staff and managers trained to identify service-oriented people?
  2. Are your selection methods aiding the process and are they themselves people-oriented?
  3. Does the process leave a good image of your company even with those who fail to get a job with you?
  4. Are promises kept in terms of letting people know the outcomes of job applications?
  5. Is feedback offered to failed candidates?

- *Induction* 1. Do you have an induction programme for all new recruits; does it start immediately on appointment?
  2. Does it cover vision, the importance of service, who your customers are, or does it just cover pay and ration issues?

3. Are people introduced properly to new colleagues, their manager and other key people or are they left to find out for themselves?

If you have to answer negatively to any of these questions, you are causing problems. Failed job applicants may carry away a bad impression of your company and do the same kind of unseen damage to your reputation as dissapointed customers can do. Staff you do appoint may be off to a bad start before you have had a day's work out of them. Their organizational values may be being left to colleagues who may not always give the best context. Once they are part of the company, all the other people systems come into play:

- *Training*
  1. Is a training programme set up to ensure they acquire the appropriate knowledge and skills?
  2. Does the training cover customer awareness and handling skills as well as technical training?
  3. Is the training style and setting supportive of the aim of high quality service?
  4. Are managers and supervisors helped with the transition to their new role when promoted?
  5. Are skills periodically refreshed?
  6. Does training take place solely in organization compartments?

- *Appraisal*
  1. Does an appraisal system exist which encourages regular discussion on performance targets and achievement?
  2. Does this help to continuously motivate and develop people in the organization or is it an annual chore?
  3. Are people skilled in making it work?
  4. Do the criteria monitored fully reflect the importance of service and quality?
  5. Do those appraised see differentiated service performance recognized?

- *Promotion*
  1. Do promotions reflect success in delivering high quality at service agent, supervisor and manager level?
  2. Are decisions seen to be fair and are they discussed openly?
  3. Is feedback given to unsuccessful candidates?

- *Pay and incentives*
  1. Are jobs evaluated in a way which reflects the importance of service?
  2. Do incentive or bonus schemes reflect quality or are they productivity/quality oriented?

3. If there is performance pay, is it given for quality of performance or quantity?

- *Uniform issue*

    1. Are those in contact with customers provided with guidelines and practical help on personal presentation?
    2. Does the uniform support your people-orientation? Is the issue sufficient for the wearer always to present a clean and tidy image?

- *Policies and procedures*

    1. Are your policies and procedures oriented towards the customer or internal administrative consideration?
    2. Are the policies and procedures ones which enable staff to give service or are they obstacles to service?
    3. Are staff allowed a measure of discretion in dealing with customer problems?

- *Facilities and equipment*

    1. Do staff have the tools to do the job?
    2. Is equipment designed to make their job easy to do or does it create unnecessary difficulties?
    3. Are facilities laid out in a way which enables staff to deal with customers effectively?

The last two areas overlap with the delivery systems included as material aspects of service, but they should be audited from a staff point of view as well. The audit is likely to show a number of areas which require corrective action. Few are likely to be expensive to put right, but may be very damaging to your service strategy if they are not attended to. They should be audited at regular intervals to maintain standards. Corrective action should involve staff as they are the users or recipients of the people systems.

9

What went wrong?

Chapter 1 contained some everyday examples of service going wrong. Let's now go back to those examples and establish likely causes. This is something which every organization should do on a regular sample basis from its customer complaints. We shall use the model which was given earlier and whose output part is set out as a reminder in Figure 9.1.

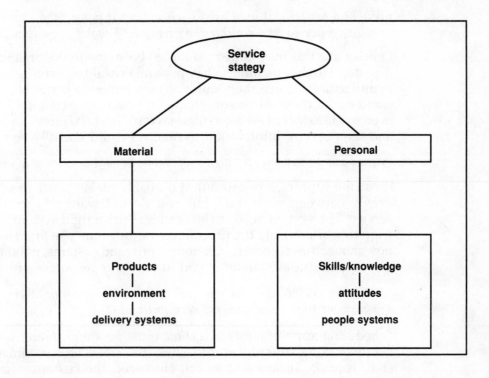

Figure 9.1   Part of the service strategy model

The electricity board will only indicate morning or afternoon – and then probably turn up in the opposite half day to that agreed.

Delivery systems are at fault here since visits cannot be scheduled to meet customer requirements. A precise appointment will be important to some, not to others. A more flexible system is therefore required. Telephone staff and service engineers are protected by the present system from having their efficiency assessed.

Whenever I ring up I get passed from phone to phone.

This is a problem of attitudes: the failure to recognize that every caller is a customer or potential customer. The customer didn't design and probably doesn't understand the organization! It may also be a knowledge problem: not knowing how to deal with the query or who should deal with it. Finally, staff may be unskilled in dealing with telephone callers.

Customer complaints of this nature call for a full review of all of these areas. Handbooks, informative phone tests, induction programmes and properly progammed telephone systems can all contribute to improvements.

I bought a toaster – it didn't work when I got it home. The retailer said it was company policy to repair rather than replace. It took three weeks to get it back.

Policies like this may appear to make sense inside the organization – but they don't to the customer. They probably wouldn't even be backed by the manufacturer. Consumers don't always know their rights or feel able to stand up for them. So ensure that your policies are customer-orientated – even to the extent of erring in their favour. Manufacturers' product quality and their service information to retailers could usefully be reviewed.

When I asked the waiter for a glass of water, he said 'I'm sorry it's not my table.'

If you are running a restaurant, it probably makes sense to allocate tables evenly between your staff, but you do not want this to result in bad service. The system needs to be flexible. With a rigid system staff may not want to work outside the procedures or they may use them as a source of power over the customers. Customer-oriented systems, good training and the right attitudes still allow you to use your resources efficiently.

I arrived for my 9.00 appointment at the clinic and found nine others with the same appointment time – and was not seen until 10.00.

Scheduling appointments in a clinic must be a nightmare, with different doctors taking different approaches, the need to co-ordinate patients, staff, records, results and so on. However, the customer has a right to expect appointment times to be kept and, if there are delays, to be advised accordingly. Having many appointments with the same time may reflect a policy of overbooking and hedging bets. Health care is slowly waking up to the fact that consumer orientation matters.

I'm fed up with my insurance company – they kept saying my policy was in the post. When I eventually had to make a claim they lost the documents and then rejected the claim.

Insurance companies have many delivery systems – procedures, paperwork, claims departments and so on – very few of which seem to be designed with the customer in mind. Add to this the difficulty of contacting the right person, lack of knowledge by people who answer the phone and you have an insurance company which is not good to do business with. It's relatively easy to switch insurance companies but, as with banks, the view of the customer is that they're probably much the same. So customers grin and bear it. But what an opportunity for differentiation – a company which not only cares but gets it right.

I'm not very knowledgeable about cars and I felt the salesmen were laughing at me.

It's very easy for an expert to make the customer feel small, patronized or pressurized. People systems are often at fault in this kind of situation – by recruiting the wrong type of staff, giving them the wrong training and paying them for quantity rather than quality. A sales philosophy which is customer-oriented will avoid procedures (such as warranty, for instance) which make customers feel ignorant. It will also result in salespeople who believe that a customer who is being helped and given time to make a decision is actually more likely to make a purchase.

The cabin crew spent more time talking among themselves than serving the customers.

In any service situation there is often a temptation to put fun with colleagues before serving the customer. The cabin crew would have been recruited partly because they were sociable and gregarious. Professionalism means always putting the customer first – an attitudinal and training issue. Cabin crew routines may also be at fault, having been devised purely for internal efficiency, and not to handle unexpected requests by customers.

The shop assistant always has to go and ask someone else the answer to my query.

New staff have to learn the job but this is often used as an excuse for too long. Product knowledge is crucial to the credibility of staff and organization. It is, therefore, the people systems which need reviewing if this is a persistent service fault.

So often service fails for small reasons – a system which doesn't always deliver, a person with insufficient knowledge or just having a bad day. Every company must, therefore, look at its service situation – not just wait for complaints – to see where they are vulnerable, to establish where the variability in performance can occur that finally results in dissatisfied customers. The service model provides you with the questions to ask and a method for improving performance.

Summary of Part I

To devise a strategy for service you need to:

- Know your customers, their needs and satisfaction level
- Understand how service can be used to create a competitive edge
- Know why some customers choose to use your competitors
- Have a vision of how the service strategy will make a difference
- Express your core purpose in a mission statement and communicate it to your staff
- Build an organization designed to respond to the customer
- Develop systems which ensure quality of your product, service environment and delivery
- Create a climate in which staff wish to respond to customer needs and provide them with the skills and knowledge to do so.
- Establish people systems, policies and procedures which facilitate good service.

Part II
Planning and running a service programme

Introduction

In Part I the process of building a service strategy was described, emphasizing the importance of obtaining customer and competitor data on a whole range of material and personal aspects of service. This data can then be used to drive and monitor the service programmes, regularly renew energy levels and create the climate and impetus for continuous improvement. The process chain model also showed the need to audit supplier performance since an acceptable output cannot come from unacceptable inputs – whether these are externally supplied raw materials or the work of other departments. Auditing is therefore a key activity which needs to be built into the improvement process. Part II explains how to design one-off and regular snapshots, including the type of questions to ask, the methodology to use and how to use the data once you have it. It goes on to show how to incorporate these audit activities into a framework of service and quality improvement – your own Customer First programme.

Part I also stressed the need for a clear sense of direction – shared by the leaders of the organization and communicated to the whole workforce. In Part II a programme for working with a senior team to explore visions and develop a mission statement is described. It is the first step in the process of designing the coherent framework of activities which will enable your service strategy to make a real difference – a difference your customers will notice.

The coherent framework of activities is designed to produce awareness of the need to change, commitment to the process of change and an environment in which change happens. This is a complex long-term task.

We are talking about a two-year programme. Ownership and commitment at all levels of the organization, starting with management are crucial. Commitment programmes have to be designed and run and levels of commitment monitored through regular audit and reviews of quality improvement plans and achievements. Although ownership concerns everybody, the improvement programme itself will need a 'kick-start' and continual coaxing. While the ultimate champion has to be the Principal Executive Officer a senior champion or co-ordinator will be required to present the total picture, co-ordinate design and implementation of activities. Ownership can be built into the line at this early stage by creating a steering team of senior managers – a Quality Council, a Total Quality

Strategy Group or a Customer Care Steering Group. What is important is not its name but its role in terms of legitimizing and enabling the new emphasis on service.

The coherence of the activities is important: people must be able to understand how activities fit together and how they lead to achievement of the mission. The use of branding, traditionally an external marketing tool, helps to communicate the fact that a broad range of activities are all concerned with quality improvement.

The activities are designed to put the service strategy into practice – building understanding, emotional commitment and practical participation in improving service performance on a continuous basis. Improving performance requires standards of service to be defined and improvement targets set; staff trained in problem solving and innovation skills and techniques and involved in carefully selected improvement projects. The process of improvement is continually fuelled by new data, by internal audits, by customer complaints and by external audits such as QA programmes and supplier partnership programmes led by your customers. In other words, there should never be a time when improvement opportunities do not arise: there will always be unexpected variations, changes to requirements, new processes being implemented, new customer requirements to satisfy. The improvement projects need to breach traditional organizational boundaries. As the service strategy model shows, most quality problems occur in the delivery and people systems areas and these rarely have a single, clear owner. The bigger management processes cross many organizational boundaries yet still have to be improved – mechanisms for doing this have to be introduced as part of the service programme.

As the service improvement programme is to be long term, ways have to be developed for reinforcing the messages and consolidating progress. Communication systems have to be overhauled, every opportunity has to be taken to repeat key messages, and successes have to be featured to keep service quality awareness to the fore. All training programmes provide an opportunity to reinforce the principles of 'customer first' and the need to seek continuous improvement. Technical training should no longer be perceived as separate from service training, whether on the job or in a classroom. Finally, service improvements need to be recognized, rewarding individuals and teams for achievement and providing encouragement to others.

Part II concentrates on the role of the manager in implementing the service strategy and bringing about performance improvement. Deming and Juran have both stated that at least 80 per cent of quality problems are to do with systems weaknesses and bureaucracy and can only be put right through management initiated activity. Very few problems can be blamed on the workforce; it is usually the systems and processes they are asked to work with. Even apparent attitude problems often have their root cause in poor training – a largely managerial process. Management in a quality organization involves managing change for the better rather than main-taining the status quo. Key result areas for managers should reflect this as should management behaviour. Most employees take their behavioural cues from people slightly higher up in the hierarchy of the company. So quality leadership has to be widely spread. Managers have to be seen to be committed to the customer, talking to them and acting on what they say, eradicating quality problems for good and encouraging subordinates to do the same.

Managers need to produce and use their own local data on customer requirements and employee attitudes. They need to devise and communi-cate meaningful improvement plans and use these to drive personal review systems in a non-restrictive, participative manner. They should both seek and provide for their subordinates, training in change manage-ment and in customer-oriented business management. They should set up improvement projects which cross traditional barriers between depart-ments rather than protecting parochialism. They should help their people to understand causes of variation and the control processes used to minimize them. 'Customer first' will only become a reality if managers want it and work for it.

Of course, the aim of all of these activities is to create a competitive edge which will enable the organization to prosper and grow. Image is part of the service strategy model. The way an organization promotes itself, deliberately or inadvertently, gives customers, or potential customers, certain expectations against which they will judge actual performance. Improved service can become a marketing tool but timing is important. The organization must be sure that if it raises expectations, they will be fulfilled. Sustained improvement adds value to a basic product and has a market price. Customers will pay for reliably high quality.

The sternest test of a service strategy is its response to customer complaints. Part II ends by looking at systems and procedures to handle complaints effectively.

What follows is not meant as a comprehensive list of ways of creating and sustaining customer orientation. The activities discussed will not be appropriate to all cultures and circumstances. The intention is to provide a menu of options which can be mixed in various ways to achieve:

- An awareness of customer service and quality principles
- Commitment to implementing these principles throughout the organ-ization
- Regular review of data to show the differences achieved.

10
The importance of ownership

The aim, as we have said, is for service improvement to become a natural part of managing the business, and for its implementation and effects to be widely shared. But the seed from which the strategy will grow must be sown at the right time in the right way by one person – the chief executive of the organization. The campaign will probably then become the responsibility of a senior executive; organizations in which this role is taken on a part-time basis risk failure and also miss an opportunity to develop a senior executive.

Involvement from other managers is essential, with numbers depending on the size and complexity of the organization. They may form a steering group which will work with the 'customer first' initiator throughout the design and implementation stages, and perhaps beyond, as a review and enforcement body. In addition to spreading ownership, the steering group managers provide a 'fifth column' of change agents within the organization. The group may need to spend some time discussing their role as change agents and the skills they need to make changes happen, such as presentation, lobbying and persuasion skills, training other managers and so on.

Ownership now has to be spread more widely within the line structure. There are some key moments for involving other managers:

- At the research stage, ensuring their views are well represented
- Feeding back the research results using them to analyse the implications and communicate these to their own people
- Once initial design has been carried out, the chief executive can obtain managers' views and do some fine-tuning before presenting it to the rest of the organization
- In the early stages of the programme all managers can have the opportunity in a workshop to reflect on the survey results, the campaign plans, the new corporate vision and values; they can then prepare individual action plans
- By developing 'local' initiatives to support the Customer First programme managers can demonstrate their own commitment and help to promote the messages in their departments

- In conferences under the Customer First banner, managers can share successes, learn from each other and review and refresh their action plans.

Ignoring the issue of ownership and leadership will result in piecemeal activities for which managers will not get the support of their staff and in managers actively undermining the service strategy. Ownership has to be spread throughout the line, and the 'customer first' executive's aim must be to work himself out of a job!

The programmes in the rest of Part II are designed to help your company achieve and maintain a position where all your workforce – managers, front-line and support staff – are all committed to the customer and to seeking continuous improvement in customer satisfaction.

11

Where are we now?

This chapter looks at the areas in which you need data to design an appropriate service strategy. You need to gather data on a regular basis and not merely to provide initial direction for your service improvement. The areas covered are:

- Customer needs/satisfaction levels
- Competitor performance
- Supplier performance
- Employee attitudes
- Material quality
- Personal service
- Image.

Customer needs/satisfaction levels

- Who are your customers? Which of them will provide you with the most fruitful partnerships?
- What do you already know about your customer needs and levels of satisfaction?
- What industry data do you have?
- What do your complaints tell you?

>The purpose of customer surveys is to fill the gaps in your knowledge and build a platform for monitoring company performance over a period of time. You may also want to use surveys to help predict future needs of customers.<

Carried out sympathetically, the survey can provide a basis for discussions which can create better partnerships between you and your customers, so it can be worth more than the data it produces. Data on the viability of your customers' businesses can help you decide which customers are likely to help you prosper. These are the ones with which you should develop a partnership approach.

You will almost certainly need professional help to design the survey and to analyse and interpret the data. If you are seeking to establish qualitative data to give a richer picture of customer needs, objective interviewers have to be used. Managers and employees, however, can be trained to establish critical success factors by interviewing customers.

Survey options to consider are:

- Group discussions for qualitative data
- Self-completion questionnaires, largely for quantitative data
- Telephone interviewing on a structured basis
- Face-to-face interviews using a questionnaire
- A combination of more than one of the above.

The following is a sample of questions from a questionnaire personally administered by an interview team to customers leaving a catering establishment. It established areas which needed to be addressed by a subsequent training programme as well as highlighting a number of product, environment and delivery system issues:

Q Including this visit, how many times have you visited this establishment in the last year?

Q Overall, how satisfied are you with the service you have received today?
v. satisfied/satisfied/not v. satisfied/not at all satisfied

Q Thinking of cleanliness:
  a) were the tables clean?   YES/NO/DIDN'T NOTICE
  b) were the serving areas clean?   YES/NO/DIDN'T NOTICE
  c) were the cutlery and crockery clean?   YES/NO/DIDN'T NOTICE

(If NO at any stage, probe for specifics)

Q About the service provided by staff, rate 1 – 5 against the following statements about staff. 5 would be the highest score, 1 the lowest. Circle x if you didn't notice/don't know.
  a) Competent
  b) Neat and tidy
  c) Warm and welcoming
  d) Apparently happy in their job
  e) Aware of you as an individual
Probe if any comments on individual staff are offered.

Q Were you thanked for your custom?   YES/NO/CAN'T REMEMBER

Q Finally, thinking of the service you have received here today, would you come back?   YES/NO/DON'T KNOW

The following is part of a questionnaire designed to establish strengths and weaknesses of delivery performance, asking respondents to compare with the perceived best competitor. In some cases the best perceived competitor was in a different industry. The customer, however, compared delivery performance with the very high standards delivered by this competitor.

AVAILABILITY	COMPANY	BEST COMPETITOR
Ordering system	5 4 3 2 1 *	5 4 3 2 1 *
Invoicing system	5 4 3 2 1 *	5 4 3 2 1 *
Ability to supply speedily on demand	5 4 3 2 1 *	5 4 3 2 1 *
Accuracy of deliveries	5 4 3 2 1 *	5 4 3 2 1 *
Communication on changes in delivery arrangements	5 4 3 2 1 *	5 4 3 2 1 *
Avoidance of damage	5 4 3 2 1 *	5 4 3 2 1 *
Working relations with distribution department	5 4 3 2 1 *	5 4 3 2 1 *
Ease of contact with sales office	5 4 3 2 1 *	5 4 3 2 1 *

5 = Excellent
4 = Above Average
3 = Average
2 = Below average
1 = Very poor
* = No opinion/not applicable

Other factors covered in the questionnaire were:

- Accessibility
- Product innovation
- Knowledge of customer's business
- Technical support, etc.

At this point you may wish to re-read Chapter 3 to remind yourself of the paramount importance of customer data and the options available to you for obtaining and using it.

Competitor performance

While the customer survey can often be used to chart competitor performance as seen by the customer, it is also wise to carry out other types of competitor analysis. Questions to be addressed are:

- Who are your key competitors?
- What are their strengths and weaknesses?

- Where do you have competitive advantage?
- What are they doing which you could do better?
- Why are some customers choosing a competitor in preference to or as well as yourselves?

A competitor audit can be carried out in most service industries. Try their products and services, ask your customers about best competitor practices, see what partnerships they are developing. British Airways had a strategy regularly to assess the competitive threats in the marketplace, eventually involving this aspect in its staff programme 'To be the best' (see Chapter 21).

Do you have a policy towards trying your competitor's products and services? A recent European survey by Management Centre Europe of one thousand executives showed that 40 per cent of their companies did not have such a policy, yet Tom Peters talks of the need for 'creative swiping' and the Japanese have always copied and improved.

Supplier performance

Any organization which is pursuing quality improvement, must consider the quality of service it is getting from its suppliers. The necessity to do this is clear, but there are various ways of going about it. Vendor questionnaires do not always get a favourable response (or any response at all), yet if you have a lot of suppliers it may initially be the only way to set quality standards for them. Setting specifications in face-to-face discussions, then monitoring performance together, creates and enhances supplier partnerships. QA programmes like ISO9000 strongly encourage you to set up supplier quality assurance procedures and your successful accreditation may depend on them. However, you do not need to be pursuing ISO9000 or equivalents to talk to your suppliers about quality. Marks & Spencer, with its high reputation for quality, has for years imposed rigid quality standards on its suppliers.

The following are examples of issues you might wish to discuss and agree with your suppliers:

- Control over the quality of raw materials against clear specifications and tolerances
- Consistent operation of processes and control of variables
- Procedures for storage, handling and dispatch of raw materials
- Development of a QA system, including the regular provision of statistical data
- Joint monitoring and measurement
- How corrective action will take place
- Penalties for quality shortfall.

Collecting data on this basis is a first step to implementing programmes such as 'Just in Time' and 'Materials Resource Planning'* which require reliable systems and data to be in place before they can be introduced.

Employee attitudes

It is important to know about staff attitudes. What do employees for instance think of:

- The company's objectives
- Customer service performance
- Communications
- How they are managed
- The amount of influence they have
- The quality of their training.

How big is the gap between employee and customer perceptions of what is important in the service situation, or between staff and management perceptions of the way the organization is run?

Again, professional help is usually required in designing, carrying out and reporting on the findings. Focus group discussions and/or questionnaires are the most used techniques, although other techniques, such as repertory grid interviewing and critical incident analysis, can tell us a lot about the interaction of staff in the service situation. A mixture of quantitative and qualitative methods provides the different kinds of information you need in dealing with cultural issues.

Below are examples of questions designed to elicit staff's views in some of the above areas. In any employee audit, it is important to be sure about its objectives and to anticipate the impact the data will have on employee relations. Questions can then be specifically designed.

COMMUNICATION

• I am well informed about company plans	1	2	3	4	5
• I am well informed about departmental plans	1	2	3	4	5
• I get enough information to do my job properly	1	2	3	4	5
• Managers take notice of employees' views	1	2	3	4	5

* Just in Time is a system to eliminate waste, minimize set-up, create shorter lead-times and better product flow. Materials Resource Planning is a system of managing all the resources of a manufacturing company. It is a set of computer supported planning and scheduling tools.

- I am fully involved in changes affecting my work   1   2   3   4   5
- The staff newspaper contains nothing but company propaganda   1   2   3   4   5

PEOPLE SYSTEMS

- I feel well trained for the work that I do   1   2   3   4   5
- Training by company trainers is more effective than by external trainers   1   2   3   4   5
- My immediate superior is concerned for my career development   1   2   3   4   5
- Graduates are unreasonably favoured   1   2   3   4   5
- The company has an effective system for assessing my performance   1   2   3   4   5

CUSTOMER SERVICE

- Getting it right for the customer is the most important thing to my manager   1   2   3   4   5
- The company has a good understanding of the needs of our customers   1   2   3   4   5
- My department provides an effective service to other departments within the company   1   2   3   4   5

1 = strongly disagree
2 = slightly disagree
3 = neither agree nor disagree
4 = slightly agree
5 = strongly agree

COMPANY/JOB

- Overall how would you rate your company as an organization to work for?   1   2   3   4   5

1 = One of the best
2 = Above average
3 = Average
4 = Below average
5 = One of the worst
* = No opinion

- What are the things you like best about working for the company?

There are many other areas which can be covered qualitatively according to what you wish to achieve from the survey and what you intend to do with the data. These include:

- Relationships with other departments
- Views of management effectiveness

- Recruitment and induction
- Social/environmental conditions
- Knowledge of company objectives
- Consultative machinery.

Professional help will be needed in designing, analysing and interpreting all but the simplest employee survey. You have to plan very carefully how you intend to use and respond to the wealth of data produced, so that the process enhances – rather than inhibits – the required changes.

Along with the customer and competitor data, the information from the staff attitude survey is crucial to the design of a custom-built service strategy, enabling the culture of the company to be changed to support customer orientation while taking staff along with the change. It shows you what the key inhibitors are to giving good service, as perceived by the staff. It's those inhibitors which have to be removed if staff are to commit themselves to the Customer First way of life.

It may also be appropriate to acquire separate data on the views of senior managers. It is important to know where managers stand if they are to own and commit themselves to the service strategy and its implementation. Headings under which data could usefully be collected are:

- Who they see as the customers
- The importance of service and quality in priority terms
- Criteria for effective service and quality management
- Other pressures vying for attention
- Effectiveness of communication
- How well the senior team functions
- Training received/required
- Benefits of a service or quality programme
- Reactions to employee survey data.

These data should preferably be collected and analysed by an external consultant used to working with senior members of an organization or through a structured questionnaire. Managers often take the opportunity to give very frank views, particularly if they are assured anonymity.

Material quality

The material aspects of service were explored in Chapter 7. Here we look at some of the basic items which need to be audited as part of a service improvement programme.

There is little chance of a service strategy producing long-term benefit if the basic quality of product is wrong or it is sub-standard packaging; or if the distribution system lets you down, or any part of the sequence of activities from order reception through to delivery fails to work. Good personal service can sometimes save the situation but not without short-term and long-term cost. Finally, a poor quality service environment throws doubt on all other aspects of your business: 'If this is how they keep their premises, I wonder if their production methods are sloppy too.'

Information about material quality will be produced by the customer research and possibly by the staff attitude survey. However, it is important to create an ongoing critical approach to material quality so that the service strategy becomes, and is generally perceived to be, a way of life rather than a 'flavour of the month'. An objective review of these material aspects is therefore important, although it need not be done in detail before the programme commences. Carrying out an audit and fixing the key areas should be an ongoing part of the programme, involving staff whose work relates to these areas. The aim of implementing a service quality programme is to establish a climate in which there is a continuous search for improvement.

To assess your strengths and weaknesses in material quality you can do the following:

- Check whether you have specifically stated standards of performance. Are they known to everybody? Are you monitoring actual performance against these standards? How do you take corrective and preventive action based on the data? Is accountability clear, even if it is shared?
- Review customer complaints. How many of them refer to material aspects of service?
- Look at inspection data. How much re-work is being done? How much waste is there? Although you may be stopping poor quality getting to the customer, there may be a lot of effort consumed by this – effort that could more profitably be used in expanding the business.
- Carry out a 'cost of quality' exercise where you list all the resources which are employed in putting right non-conformance and all the resources put into assuring conformance. You will probably underestimate the costs but it will give you an idea of the prize available to a high quality operation. Cover all parts of the business, including the central/support services, such as:

  - Customer complaints – compensation and handling time
  - Incorrect delivery of orders/invoice mismatches; re-deliveries
  - Purchase order changes
  - Scrapping of raw materials
  - Inadequately maintained equipment
  - Frequent design reviews
  - Unplanned plant/equipment down time
  - Not manufacturing to customer specification
  - Re-work/down grades

- Contamination from dirty containers/process machinery
- Double handling in warehouse
- Poor housekeeping
- Excessive programme testing and debugging
- Late delivery/installation
- Poor/inaccurate/late point-of-sale material
- Ineffective recruitment procedures
- Meetings with ill defined agendas/timescales.

Measurement enables you to promote awareness of efficiency and waste, and to show where improvement has taken place. The cost of catching failure before it reaches the customer should come down to the much smaller cost of preventing poor quality in the first place.

- Audit the service environment. How does it look – is it clean, tidy, spacious? Is it designed for customers or for your own convenience? Ask your staff how if affects their work. Ask the customers what they like or dislike about it. This is particularly important for shops, restaurants, take-away outlets, car dealerships, leisure facilities, banks, building societies, hospitals, doctor's surgeries and jobcentres. It is also important in manufacturing companies to review reception areas, distribution pick-up points, depots and so on as this is where customers or their agents make their judgements about you as a company.
- Carry out a critical review of your service system – from your customers' point of view. Walk through the service experience with a staff member and a customer. Get a feel for what really happens, not what ought to happen. Find out where the systems are most vulnerable, where the bottlenecks are, and which systems are consistently serving a useful purpose.

Personal service

You will obtain a wealth of data about personal service from your customer research and internal service, teamwork and communication from your employee attitude survey. Any factor which is revealed to be preventing staff from providing good service to customers must be attended to. Staff cannot give of their best to customers if they feel they are not getting good service themselves from within the company.

As the service model in Chapter 2 indicated, there needs to be an objective internal review of the personal aspects of service to see why the weaknesses exist and to generate corrective action. The review must involve:

- Checking whether clear performance standards exist and have been communicated and understood; checking that the standards reflect customer not organizational needs
- Reviewing procedures and documentation to ensure that they support, not inhibit customer service. If staff are constantly having to bend them to fit the situation then they need amending or scrapping. Examples might be:

  - Forms which ask for data which is not essential (eg many hotel registration forms)
  - Organizing work in a way which requires a customer to queue twice to help your accounting procedures
  - Documentation with jargon and codes which confuse the customer
  - Small print which removes liability for service received (eg a 48-hour service response which really means six eight-hour days)
  - Rules which prohibit staff from agreeing small amounts of compensation which would defuse a situation.

  Some of these may also have been identified by your walk-through with a customer, recommended as part of your material service audit procedures.

- Reviewing training programmes; are the key skills/knowledge areas being taught well (or at all)? Is 'sitting by Nelly' just perpetuating faults and bad habits? Is training supporting or inhibiting good service? Are the right attitudes being instilled in new recruits right from the start? Is the learning technology itself responsive enough to the needs of the organization to allow faster learning, nearer to the workplace?
- Check out your recruitment and selection criteria. Is the service value incorporated? How effective are your induction procedures? Do any of your payment systems reflect productivity or quantity to the detriment of quality? Are your managers assessed in terms of managing service quality?

Not all of these areas need to be audited before your service campaign commences, but will be given priority by managers in the programme of initiatives described in Chapter 13.

The data received from all the surveys and audits described so far are vital as they illustrate the gaps between where you'd like to be as a service organization and where your customers and employees see you. They also reveal your competitive position in the marketplace and best practice in other service companies. It is important that the data are used firstly to explain the need for a service strategy, and then to set out its direction. Any launch programme, awareness or training programmes will refer to these data and drive fix-it and innovation activities. New or revised standards and monitoring methods will all be based on survey and audit data. Without the audits covered in this chapter, any service programme is to a large degree, 'shooting in the dark', and cannot expect to develop a market-oriented, customer-responsive, high quality organization.

Image audit

The image of a company in the marketplace is a combination of many factors in addition to the quality of its customer service. These factors must be reviewed to see if they support or inhibit the service intentions of the organization. The following are some of the questions you might ask:

- Is your livery reflecting the service orientation – does it represent a caring image or an impersonal one? Even the colours used can suggest coolness or warmth. Do staff uniforms help the warm and friendly service image of a high quality organization or do they look austere or untidy or old fashioned. A change of uniform may be an outward sign of intention to change service image. Vans which are dirty, posters which are torn, signs in the old livery are all indicators of a poor quality organization
- How are you projecting the company through advertising, promotions and public relations activity? Are you living up to the image you are portraying? Does your promotional activity support your internal service improvement or is it becoming a hostage to fortune?
- When recruiting and selecting staff are opportunities taken to enhance the quality image of the company – good brochures, prompt responses, personalized letters and so on. Do you leave failed candidates with a positive or negative image of your company?

Reputation is often based on perception and secondhand information rather than fact, so it is important to check whether your picture of the way the company does its business matches the way the outside world sees it.

If your research and audits have shown weaknesses in your service performance, don't make service a central plank of your promotional activity. When you are confident of your performance and you know the customers are noticing, then you can use your improved service as a promotional device (see Chapter 16).

Again, not all the audit work needs to be completed before launching a service campaign as the audit can be an ongoing part of the programme of involving staff – in this case marketing, public relations and personnel staff in particular.

So auditing or taking regular snapshots is important in all of the areas covered. Some of it needs to be done initially to direct your service strategy, the rest becomes an integral part of your implementation plan, using the front-line staff to audit performance and fix the weaker areas, involving appropriate support staff where system or procedure changes are needed. In any service strategy, data form your most important weapons and particularly data about what the customer believes is important. Having real data means that you don't have to theorize about the need for service quality; the evidence is provided by customers and staff. This reduces defensiveness and increases ownership.

12

Visions and values

We have talked so far about developing management ownership and commitment to a service improvement strategy which will be based on data generated by a comprehensive audit process. We have seen the need for vision expressed as a corporate philosophy or mission statement.

The following is an outline two-day programme for a senior team to work on vision and mission, to establish priorities for change and to discover the barriers to achieving such change. It is a programme which can be repeated lower down the organization using the statements developed by the senior team as a framework. At a senior level it is vital to use a facilitator from outside the company. The role of the facilitator is described later.

Day One

Introductions

Explanation of terms

Vision exercise

Strengths and weaknesses of service performance

Gap analysis

Day Two

Defining a mission

Setting out the key values

Transition

Communicating the mission

Instilling the corporate values

Personal action planning

A fuller explanation of each part of the programme follows.

DAY ONE

Introductions	– why we are here, what we hope to achieve, the role of the facilitator, the group process
Explanation of terms	– vision, mission, values, objectives, targets and the purpose of a vision exercise as a precursor to cultural change
Vision exercise	– a blue skies approach; use of words, symbols or pictures to depict the ideal future state. This may cover headings such as:

– stance towards the marketplace
– people development
– quality of life
– community responsibility
– the way you want to do business
– the way you want to be perceived, etc

Participants should be encouraged to have fun breaking away from traditional patterns of thought. Ask them to think of other companies and organizations they admire and to assess what it is they do differently. Ask them to concentrate on customer service and test out the vision statements – will they ensure improved customer service. Can a customer charter be developed from the vision – a set of delivery statements which you would aspire to and would be prepared to be judged by?

Strength and weaknesses	– It is now important to get a clear picture of the current situation, taking stock of what you are good at (with evidence to support) and areas that need improvement. This can be done as a syndicate flip-chart exercise in two parts, listing strengths first and then weaknesses.
Gap analysis	– Compare the 'stock taking' findings with your vision of the future and establish the gaps that have to be bridged. Describe these gaps in a way which illustrates the changes needed and how you will know when you have successfully achieved the changes. The external facilitator can help with the objectivity of this analysis. The time between Day One and Day Two will enable the analysis to be reviewed and professionally presented on Day 2.

DAY TWO

Defining a mission	– Putting the core purpose of the enterprise into words, based on the vision exercise of the previous day. Drafting in committee can be a problem, so a facilitator or volunteer should be used to draft a version for subsequent improvement by the senior team.
Setting out the key values	– Defining organizational values is often the start of significant cultural change. Here is an opportunity for the senior team to discuss how they will express these new values in practice as well as their general impact on organizational behaviour.
Transition/ Communicating mission/ Instilling corporate values	– A debate about the most difficult aspect of the change – making plans to help people understand the nature of the mission, how the values work out in practice and what will be expected of staff. Remember, one man's vision is often another man's threat.
Personal action planning	– What is each member of the senior team going to do to demonstrate personal commitment to the mission and the new corporate values. How will they promote understanding of the vision and the changes it entails in their own departments?

The external facilitator is helpful in four ways:

- Initiating objective senior team debates
- Processing and presenting back the data generated during the programme – again, in an objective way
- Drafting the mission statement for discussion
- Helping individuals to develop action plans for their units.

Once the senior team have communicated the output of their session, they can lead similar exercises in each of their departments and hence start the process of giving a clear direction for the future to each department. The mission statements can then be reflected in individual managers' key result areas (see Chapter 15) and start to have a real effect on the performance of the organization.

The vision becomes a vital piece of communication in launching the service improvement programme. If its contents are undisputed, and it is presented with passion it provides a firm foundation for generating interest, enthusiasm and involvement. Ambiguity and insincerity can undermine the whole change programme.

Communicating the mission to the whole workforce to gain their commitment to a common cause must be very carefully planned. The following chapter shows how achieving this is fundamental to the whole service initiative.

13

Launching a service programme

This chapter covers the main elements you are likely to require during the first 12 to 18 months of your service initiative. It shows how to design appropriate programmes and implement them as part of a coherent plan of action. It starts by highlighting the need to use creative communication techniques to capture and maintain interest.

Marketing the message

We need to 'think marketing' instead of using more traditional approaches to employee communication. The fact that we are talking about an internal campaign to start with, does not mean that there is no need for style, attention grabbing, humour and colour – all the techniques taken for granted in selling to outside customers. The staff are the customers of this programme and need to be approached as such.

The programme will benefit from having a theme; a good theme will evoke action, it will remain fresh and apt throughout, and it will encapsulate the whole purpose of the service strategy. A logo can add interest and give a 'brand' identity to the various activities. British Airways campaign was called Putting the Customer First, and the staff teams were called Customer First Teams. The logo shown in Figure 13.1 emphasized the customer/staff relationship.

A coherent framework

Each programme will have a range of activities covering commitment, training, communication, involvement, reinforcement and so on, depending on the overall aims, the maturity of the culture and the resources available. Activities must be planned, at least in outline, and form a coherent framework which allows each one to make sense on its own and also as a contributory part. If they are not presented in this way, they will not make sense to employees who will label them halfbaked, piecemeal, 'flavour of the month'. Much better that employees should feel involved in a comprehensive and coherent set of activities aimed at delivering high quality service to the customer.

Figure 13.1 Company logos used in Customer First campaigns

The service strategy model in Chapter 2 provides a way of establishing how strongly focused your organization is on the customer. The surveys and the vision exercise are carried out prior to commencement of a wider service campaign and should, ideally, provide the data for the design and selling of such a campaign. Many campaigns of this nature appear to have common elements, illustrated in the framework in Figure 13.2.

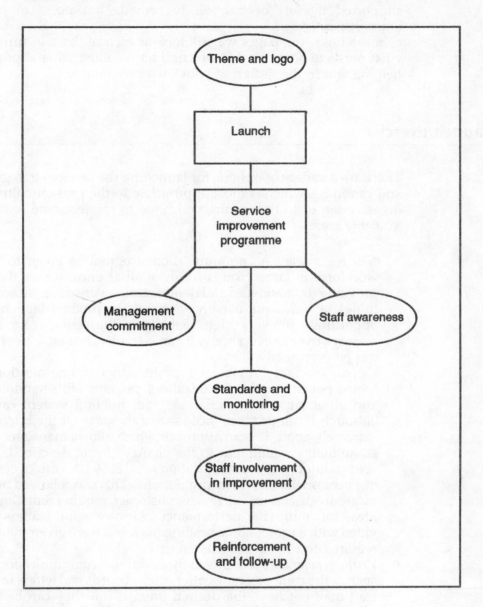

Figure 13.2   Typical service strategy framework of activities

The theme and logo are used to brand all the activities, including the launch exercise, to show that something new, interesting and different is going on. The map of activities shows the seriousness and long-term nature of the initiative, getting managers committed first, building staff awareness, then using standards, monitoring and staff involvement supported by lots of training to provide a process of continuous improvement.

In the following pages we will look at each of these in turn, showing what needs to be covered in practical terms, illustrating approaches and helping you in the design of your own programme.

Launch exercise

There are a variety of options for launching the service strategy and only you can judge which is most appropriate to the present culture of your organization or to the culture you hope to create. Some of the options available are:

- *'The big splash'*: A communication programme given to the whole workforce in large groups (or even all at once) where the aim is to provide a dramatic start and demonstrate a very different way of doing things; a technique usually reserved for product launches. It's an opportunity for very high visibility of the senior team and gets a message over to everybody. It can be costly, but on a 'per head' basis can be very good value.
- *Cascade briefing:* Providing a professional communication package which penetrates the organization, perhaps with handouts, videos and other support material. A team briefing system can be ideal although it can produce inconsistent messages if the briefers are not extremely good. It is an approach which allows managers to demonstrate their commitment to the changes being described. ICI Paints sent an important communication to all 3000 UK employees to launch its Focus on the Customer programme. This was followed by a cascade of group discussion to review customer requirements and develop ideas for improving performance. All discussion leaders were provided with a professional briefing pack and were given training where required to run their Focus groups.
- *Written communication:* The more traditional communication methods, such as the company newsletter, noticeboards and letters to individual staff may not have the desired impact. But they can be used most effectively as support devices to either of the above methods.

Remember, the service strategy is designed to create a difference, so start with one!

In terms of content the communication programme needs to cover a range of messages, at least in outline. Topics must include:

- *Vision/mission:* What does the senior team want the organization to look like in future? What are the key values it wishes to espouse? What changes will it result in and what will be required from each of them?
- *Survey results:* What you have established about the customers' needs and levels of satisfaction: how you rate against the competition; where staff stand in terms of service and what they think are the inhibitors; where your weaknesses are in systems and procedures. In other words, this is an opportunity to say what you do well and what you have to improve to meet the customers' needs.
- *Aims of service:* What you hope to achieve.
- *Strategy:* What is the prize for reaching it and how you intend to measure progress. Above all, what's in it for each and every employee? The marketplace, competitive threats and future industry trends may provide a useful backcloth and illustrate why service and quality must become such important parts of your business strategy.
- *Programme of activities:* The communication programme gives you the opportunity to present the action plan, outlining activities, their aims and timescales and how each individual is to be involved. The theme and logo can be introduced, demonstrating a coherent approach. Audio visual presentations can be used effectively here.
- *Summary:* Restatement of the key messages, activities, benefits and expectations, and a reminder that there is no opting out for anyone; and there is no alternative to making quality and service key strategic issues.

Management commitment programme

A service strategy will stand or fall by the seriousness with which the managers of the organization view it. It is essential, therefore, to broaden ownership beyond the dedicated group designing and planning implementation at all stages. Lobbying of their colleagues by this group is an important way to nurture enthusiasm and ownership, but the activities must all be designed to get responsibility for service quality firmly in the hands of line management. The programme should never be seen by managers as a threat. They must see the contribution it can make, and this requires some at least of the following:

- *Researching their views:* This was suggested as part of the audit phase. It not only helps to pinpoint potential blockages but also develops a degree of commitment and involvement. Ascertain managers' reactions to survey findings through interactive presentations and elicit their views on what collective action needs to be taken.

71

- *Consultation:* At key stages test the design, using managers' views to improve it, tell them what you have done, and discuss the implications for them.
- *Briefing:* Once final plans are in place, devise a programme to explain them to managers. Make sure they understand the purpose, the logistics and the implications for their staff. Put together a slide-show and get the design team to take it round to every management team. It should be a persuasive presentation which stimulates debate and challenges cynicism as it arises. Put the programme into their context, show how they can use it as a vehicle to make change happen in their area.
- *Vision exercise:* It may be appropriate to run vision exercises for each department using the corporate one as the starting point. A clear statement will help to focus the whole department. At a departmental level a mission becomes the foundation stone for defining management objectives or key result areas against which specific quality- or service-related targets can be set and measured. It also shows which managers are enthusiastic about customer service and which are only paying it lip service.
- *Change management:* To support the type of cultural change necessary, a more in-depth programme for managers will be required as a key part of the service initiative. This should be designed to help them audit their own role as quality managers, build on their strengths and set action plans to correct weaknesses. Skills of listening, briefing and counselling, and an understanding of the nature of change should be central to this programme. Techniques such as 'domainal mapping' can help the managers audit their own performance, and 'force field analysis' can enhance the effectiveness of their action plans. Discussion on company culture, the survey findings and certain audit findings can be used to trigger commitment to making change happen. If the personal review or management objectives systems are being re-focused on customer service and internal quality, then appraisal skills may need to be refreshed within either this or a related programme.

  Robb Wilmot, the man who turned round ICL, has said that British managers are around two weeks short on training every year. The launch of a major service strategy provides an opportunity to create a practical, meaningful programme to fill this void.

  Chapters 14 and 15 show how training for staff and managers is an essential part of the strategy for continuous improvement in customer relations.
- *Launch:* Managers should be involved in announcing the service campaign. Ensure they do it professionally – well scripted and rehearsed, if necesssary, as it is their first opportunity to reveal the change the company wishes to undergo, and staff will be watching keenly to see how well they do it, and how committed they are.

Staff awareness programmes

The launch programme will generate awareness of the need for improved quality of performance, and the plan of activities, set out under the action logo, should be an exciting prospect for staff.

However, full understanding will only come about through a series of carefully constructed pieces of communication and involvement over a period of time. British Airways' Putting People First (PPF) was designed specifically to address one of the corporate objectives – to create a people- and service-oriented environment. However, it became just the first of a whole series of training programmes which contributed greatly to a common understanding throughout the workforce.

The main elements of PPF, other than its content were:

- It was a totally new departure, and a dramatic sign of the organization's re-found commitment to people (particularly necessary following the redundancy and retrenchment programme).
- It mixed staff from all disciplines, enabling them for the first time to debate interface issues in a relaxed but structured way and it was, therefore, an overt corporate teambuilding approach.
- By focusing on personal development it demonstrated an investment in people themselves and it was their choice whether they used this investment to further British Airways' interest or merely to improve their own quality of life. In most cases both benefited at least to some degree.
- The event itself had the hallmark of quality and this was quite deliberately designed into every aspect of the two days.

British Airways was a pioneer of large-scale motivational training, and other companies creating their own staff awareness programmes can learn from BA's experience. The following elements could be considered in programmes designed to trigger the processes of communication and participation required to make service quality a way of life for everybody in the organization.

- *Customer responsiveness:* Explaining why the organization needs to become more responsive to the customer, how this is brought about by the combination of people and service systems to create the many 'moments of truth'. Where survey data have been obtained, they can be used creatively to stimulate understanding and a new approach to customers. Discussing customer complaints and debating how situations might have been better handled, can add richness to this debate.
- *Customer service:* The elements of good service practice, exploring the relationship between material and personal aspects of service, looking at specific service situations and options for handling them, showing

that service is largely an emotional experience based on many factors, but particularly influenced by interaction with front-line staff.

- *Quality:* Showing the importance of internal quality in terms of product, safety, environment and delivery systems, focusing on the people without direct customer contact who make these material aspects happen, links with quality initiatives in the organization. Exploring what quality means in terms of individual responsibility and broadening to discussions of the quality of working life, explaining the rewards brought about through a philosophy of continuous improvement.

- *The concept of the internal customer:* Organizational structures tend to be designed with internal efficiency rather than customer needs in mind. This can only be remedied by staff working effectively across the boundaries between departments. The concept of the internal customer means everybody in an enterprise having a customer for their work. Accounts, personnel, purchasing, engineering and management services all have internal customers. Understanding internal customers' needs and establishing how well they are being satisfied ensures that each part of the chain, working with the other parts, is providing the very best for the paying customer. The message is: 'If you're not serving the customer then you'd better be serving someone who is.' Data from an employee survey will be useful in this session. Meeting in mixed groups on the programme is itself a way of improving understanding of how parts of the organization fit together. The session is encapsulated in the following statement: 'The quality of service provided to the customers starts with the service people inside the organization give to each other.'

- *Personal development:* Whole books have been written on this subject, and there are some topics which are particularly relevant to giving service and which can be built into the training programme:

  - body language
  - transactional analysis
  - 'strokes' and attention
  - winners, confidence, assertive behaviour
  - owning the problem.

Exploring these aspects of attitude and behaviour in the context of customer service and teamwork leads to a greater recognition of individual responsibility for producing quality and the personal rewards which result in improved performance.

- *Improvement techniques:* Depending on length and purpose of the programme, there may be an opportunity to cover some techniques for solving problems and generating ideas. Brainstorming in small groups to show the potential for grassroot problem solving, plus some simple prioritizing techniques, can be the basis for more comprehensive involvement activities later on. These could be quality circles, action teams or one-off project teams (see p.84). The concept of continuous improvement must certainly be explored.

The content and style of the awareness programme must take account of the existing culture of the organization, while demonstrating the new values,such as openness and honesty, for instance. The kind of changes required can be indicated during opening and closing sessions by a member of the senior team, by attendance of managers on the programme, by forums built into the design, and by follow-up of issues raised.

Other questions to be considered in the design are:

- Cost/budget available
- External or internal presenters or both
- Venue availability/quality
- Length of programme
- Size of groups
- Group mix
- Media/materials.

The greatest impact can be achieved if the whole organization experiences the programme, mixed across all disciplines and levels, managers and staff on the same programme. Group size may depend on release constraints and the time it takes to get a critical mass of people interested and keen for a dramatic impact on the organization to be made. Large group events are themselves a dramatic change from traditional training activity and they require specialist expertise which may not be readily available within an organization. However, it can be developed over a period of time, as shown by the British Airways programmes which followed up Putting People First. These were hosted by volunteer BA staff who were given some initial coaching and support but very quickly ran the whole programme. Many other organizations are now running similar programmes. The length of the programmes varies according to content, but as their aim is awareness and not skill development, one or two days is usual. A one-day programme can be effective if it is part of a carefully conceived framework of activities and is understood to be such. On its own it should not be seen as the principal change device.

Venue is another important factor, decided by group size, geographical spread and, of course, availability. The logistics are very complex; a dedicated team is needed to ensure everything happens as planned. In British Airways most of the programmes were run at an in-house Heathrow venue which was refurbished to give the quality of venue required. This was far more cost-effective than hiring hotel conference facilities, and it provided an uprated facility for many other uses.

Lloyds Bank and Volkswagen Audi Group (VAG) UK, with their audiences spread across the UK, had to devise roadshows. Lloyds imposed a maximum travel time which made scheduling an even more challenging task.

Whatever the choice of venue, it must provide a quality environment – both materially and personally – to support the messsage of the programme itself. Hotel or in-house catering staff need to be briefed on the purpose of the programme, as they become the immediate research ground for an audience thinking about quality and service. Properly briefed, they can become an integral part of the event – and benefit from it themselves.

The style of the programme also has to demonstrate the same message: high quality reception and presentations, opportunities for interaction and participation must all be built in. Day-long lectures would not reflect the new values. Speakers have to be interesting, amusing, challenging and very responsive to the members of what may be a large audience. None of this is easy yet it is by these criteria that the seriousness of the whole initiative will be judged. Quality audio visual material, used sparingly, will enhance: music and pictures can bring the organization and its marketplace to life. It is exciting for individuals in the audience to be able to look at a slide or video and say 'that's my work up there!'

Training materials can be produced to support the programme and provide an opportunity to illustrate a quality approach different from traditional courses which delegates will previously have attended. These materials should be designed to stimulate interest and enthusiasm during the programme and remain useful afterwards.

A quality awareness programme is never cheap. With large attendances some of the costs are spread, but there are per head costs which cannot be reduced – materials, tutor fees, venue hire, catering. A one-day programme in an in-house venue may cost as little as £35 per head, whereas a two-day residential programme in a hotel may cost up to £150. In terms of the entire organization's finances, the cost may be similar to the cost of supplying free coffee to everyone for a year, it may be 0.1 per cent of the year's expenditure or 1 per cent of profit. Whichever way it is presented, it is an investment which can be extremely well rewarded by better service in the marketplace and improved internal relationships.

The following awareness programme in a small UK health authority led straight into problem solving and innovation during an action-packed day.

ASPIRING TO EXCELLENCE
PEMBROKESHIRE HEALTH AUTHORITY

PLENARY
  Objectives of programme
  Introductions
  Achievements to date
  Why customers?
  Teamwork

ROTATING WORKSHOPS
Communications Factor
 reviewing findings of staff survey and working on improvement ideas
Systems Factor
 identifying systems which inhibit good service and working on action plans
Human Factor
 our behaviour affects the behaviour of those we interact with; good service guide
Customer Factor
 a fun exercise to present ideas on how to spend £100,000 on improving service to customers; an exercise in allocating scarce resources

PLENARY
Presentations from all the syndicates
Hot seat interview with the District General Manager.

The ideas identified at the workshops are prioritized and implemented wherever possible or put to a staff *'Focus Group'* to take a more considered review and prepare an implementation plan for presentation to management.

Setting and monitoring standards

Once an awareness of customer service – both external and internal – exists at all levels and in all departments, questions start to be raised:

- How do we measure progress?
- What specifically are we trying to achieve?
- Who are our customers?
- What do our customers want?
- How do we measure quality?
- How do we best use the customer data?

Many companies generate, collate and publish data about performance, but it is often not achieving very much in terms of performance improvement. It may be unimaginatively presented, not widely communicated, or give no sense of customers' priorities. Defining standards of performance, if done well, leads to the setting of objectives and targets which are challenging and enable individual performance to be measured. This is the only way to sustain continuous improvement.

First check you know who your customers are and who the key decision makers are, these are the people with whom you should be setting your standards. You need to decide which three to five things matter most at any unit level, and only these should be measured. To define them you first have to ask your customers what is important to them in terms of being effective in their business, what are their critical success factors.

Market research may have indicated these areas, if not go and ask your customers. *Manager knows best,* behaviour is no longer good enough, only customer-led appraisal.

So, for instance, research might establish that the key areas of concern to customers are:

- Delivery accuracy
- Invoicing/order match accuracy
- Speed of answering the telephone
- Technical service response times
- Stock availability.

In some situations you may find that the customer has much better data in these areas than you do. The customer may also have the same data on your competitors and be able to let you know when you fall short of expectations. This should never be ignored and can be of most benefit to you if it is done as part of a customer partnership programme.

Possible methods of measuring the above factors could be:

- Deliveries   – % delivered on time
                    – % delivered to order specification
- Invoices   – % which match the order paperwork
- Telephones   – % answered within three rings
- Technical service   – number of calls made within 24 hours of notification
- Stock   – number of stock outs per month

Measurement of the things that really matter has to become a way of life in an organization aspiring to service excellence, so it has to be carried out at individual, departmental and corporate level if continuous improvement is to become a reality.

As employees need standards to know what they are supposed to be achieving, they must be persuasively communicated. Telephone response times, complaint handling, tolerance levels for a production process, baggage delivery targets are all technical standards which can be measured by observation on a sample basis or for every transaction. Graphs, trend data and pictures can all be used for performance improvement if they are communicated to the people required to meet the standards.

Some standards of behaviour must be set too. This is a more subjective area and one which is more difficult to monitor, but it is also one by which many customers are likely to judge your service. It cannot, therefore, be left to chance. Research into how customers wish to be treated can give valuable guidance. The standards set must form part of all skill training programmes and be monitored by supervisors as well as by directly asking customers.

As an example, British Airways' approach to this qualitative aspect of service in the specific area of check-in at Heathrow is illustrated below:

Ground Operations, London
Check-in standards

On departure

Our customers expect . . . to be treated in a courteous, helpful and professional manner:

- Greet our customers in a warm and friendly way
- Maintain eye contact
- Use our customers' names
- Make clear announcements
- Avoid jargon
- Where awkward situations occur deal with them discreetly, politely and firmly
- Give honest explanations
- Don't hesitate to apologize.

Our customers expect . . . to see British Airways presenting a good image.

- Maintain clean, tidy and attractive work areas
- Present a smart appearance at all times.

Our customers expect . . . to have their needs dealt with quickly and efficiently.

- Anticipate our customers' needs
- Be flexible and adaptable
- Give clear and helpful information
- Check understanding and summarize.

Our customers expect . . . reliable information to reassure them in areas of doubt and concern:

- Keep our customers informed
- Give reasons for delays
- Provide regular updates
- Show particular concern for the needs of the elderly, disabled and families
- Answer customers' questions clearly and concisely.

Similar standards exist for arrival. These standards were derived from a departure questionnaire carried out in the boarding area. This is part of the questionnaire used in 1985.

When you checked in for your flight, how satisfied were you with the service you received from the check-in staff? Were you:

Very satisfied
Satisfied
Not very satisfied
Not at all satisfied
Don't know

IF NOT SATISFIED: Why do you say that?

Slow service
Off-hand/rude
Unhelpful staff
Inefficient system
Not enough staff/desks
Made mistakes
Ran out of cards/tags
Lack of/little/incorrect info. given
Language problem
Inexperienced/staff didn't know what doing
Specific seats not available

Other (write in) ....

....

....

Were you addressed by name at check-in?

Yes
No
Don't know

I am going to read a series of statements and I would like you to tell me on a scale of 1 to 5 how well each describes the service you received today at check-in. A mark of 5 would be the highest score, a mark of 1 the lowest.

How would you rate the check-in staff on being . . .?

Competent	5	4	3	2	1	DK
Courteous and polite	5	4	3	2	1	DK
Showed an interest in you as an individual	5	4	3	2	1	DK
Appeared to enjoy their job	5	4	3	2	1	DK
Warm and welcoming	5	4	3	2	1	DK

Data from questions such as these are compiled into monthly reports using graphs with commentary. Two examples of graphs (using hypothetical data) are shown in Figures 13.3 and 13.4.

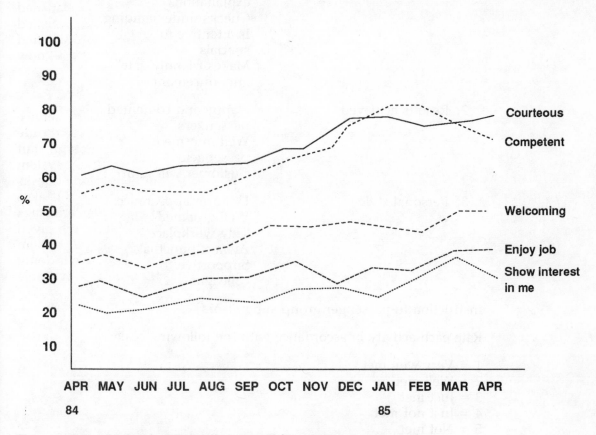

Figure 13.3   Attitude of check-in staff (% giving 5 out of 5)

The gap between competence and warmth continued to be a problem for British Airways; 'showing interest in the passenger as an individual' consistently obtained the lowest rating. All factors showed improvement, however, during the first two years of the Customer First drive and then tended to reach a plateau.

Since being addressed by name both personalizes the transaction and is a mark of respect, this became a constant area for attention, particularly in shuttle and short-haul transactions. Over time these percentages were increased.

The same areas were monitored by supervisors whose checklist also covered technical skills. Unacceptable ratings led to an agreed improvement action plan. The checklist included:

1. Customer service
Is warm and friendly
Uses customer name
Maintains eye contact
Gives clear
explanations
Checks understanding
Is attentive to
specials
Makes friendly gate
announcements

2. Results achieved
Happy and contented
passengers
Well informed
passengers
Customer will return

3. Personal style
Uniform appearance
Well groomed
Tidy workplace
Always punctual
Supportive to
colleagues

Instruction to passenger group supervisors

Rate each activity in accordance with the following scale:

1 = Very well met
2 = Well met
3 = Just met
4 = Just not met
5 = Not met
6 = Definitely not met.

If rating below 2 is given, the action plan is to be completed. Please confirm what action will be taken to improve the Agent's performance. Make particular note of further training needs.

If, as is likely at the start of the initiative, actual performance falls well below desired standards, incremental targets for improvement can be set. As targets are met, the team's or individual's achievement should be recognized and the new target announced. In Australia, ICI Dulux set a service performance index combining a number of delivery factors. Targets were set for improvement, with a sum of money for every employee each time the new target was reached. (Reinforcement and recognition is covered more fully in the next chapter.)

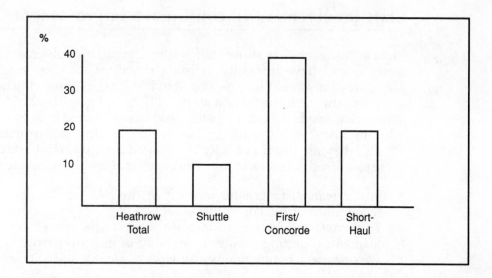

Figure 13.4 Percentage of passengers recalling that they were addressed by name

Individual objectives can also be related to achievement of standards, and management objectives to the unit's performance (see Chapter 15).

To sum up: standards are essential, but must be carefully chosen to focus attention on the things that matter to the customer. It will often be possible to agree the standards with individual customers; with internal customers this can always be done. It provides an excellent way of breaking down the organizational barriers, thus increasing internal efficiency enormously.

Standards must be well communicated to the people who have to deliver; it is worthwhile involving them in the development of standards, using the research data. Monitoring methods need to be set up and data presented in an eye-catching way to those who have to meet the standards. Big charts on a factory wall about order accuracy, breakages, lost time, safety and accidents will serve to remind everybody about what the priorities are and how performance is measuring up.

Standards must constantly be reviewed with the customer, whose needs don't stand still. It is little use monitoring something that no longer matters to the customer.

Standards and performance data should form a regular agenda item at management meetings from the board downwards, and be afforded equal importance with financial or market share data by senior management; the other two will only provide good reading if service performance is under control.

Targets and standards can be used in recognition and reward schemes, competitions between teams, and so on.

Staff involvement in continuous improvement

Most attitude surveys show staff wanting greater involvement, although many would have difficulty defining exactly what they mean by this. There are many benefits in getting staff involved in improving quality and service to the customer. For a start, staff have a great deal of knowledge about what needs to be done better, and how it should be achieved. Those who are closest to the customers have valuable information on their needs. Finally, they are often not fully challenged by their day-to-day work, so there is unused potential to tap. The benefits of involvement are therefore:

- *To the individual:* greater interest in the job; new skills developed; recognition of his contribution.
- *To the company:* better morale; utilization of the workforce; improved teamwork; getting greater ownership of improvements.
- *The customers:* better quality and service; greater understanding of their needs.

Staff involvement generates ownership of change and gets ideas implemented which would have been unthinkable if they had come from management. In most UK organizations, perhaps only 15-20 per cent of the average workforce will show an initial interest in actual involvement (even though many more may have indicated they were interested through the attitude survey). Involving these people provides quick rewards but the challenge is to attract greater commitment from the rest. This may well include, at the other end of the spectrum, 15-20 per cent of unshakeable cynics who don't believe it's their job to get involved. In the early stages it's best to leave them to it – peer pressure and the Hawthorne effect may work on them eventually.

It's also important to get the trade unions understanding that such involvement is a parallel system of communication – not one designed to replace normal consultation. There may be some managers who wish to use the service programme to impede trade union activity, but they should be warned against doing so. If shop stewards are suspicious, persuade them to get involved themselves rather than standing back as observers, which may eventually result in them becoming isolated and bitter.

Over the past few years involvement has tended to be through quality circle programmes. However, there are a number of similar techniques for handling specific issues identified as important by management, from the audit data or from the surveys. These include:

- Task forces
- Project teams
- Focus groups
- Inter-functional teams
- Corrective action teams.

Leadership can be by a senior manager or somebody from the rank and file. Team members can be chosen or volunteers. Whatever the style of group, successful involvement activities require:

- Visible commitment from senior managers
- Adaptability to organizational sub-cultures
- A supportive management framework
- Provision of training for those involved.

Visible commitment means backing the programme with resources, praising team performances, and knowing which projects are being pursued. Each company has its own culture and sub-cultures and team organization must be appropriate. A one-hour-per-week rule would be totally inappropriate for itinerant or shift workers who may have to meet less regularly but for longer. A supportive management framework enables team members to be released for meetings, and provides information and guidance. It is particularly important that issues which cross boundaries are dealt with effectively as they are the cause of most serious quality and service problems. Management may have to assist in breaking down barriers until people feel able to do this themselves.

Team leaders and team members need to be trained. Team leaders can be trained in project management, processing ideas, problem solving and so on. They can also be trained to train their groups during the early meetings and be provided with the appropriate materials during their own training programme, using simple technology such as desk top presenters or pre-prepared OHP foils or flip-charts.

An example of the content of a team leader training programme is shown below, followed by a structure for training the group during the first few meetings, as the need for the new skills arise.

Team Leader Training
Programme content

Problem identification

- Brainstorming techniques
- Barriers to thinking
- Prioritizing ideas

Systematic problem solving

- Cause and effect diagrams
- Data collection methods
- Data analysis and display techniques
- Planning implementation
- Force field analysis and other techniques

85

Presentation skills

- Structure
- Process
- Report writing

Effective meetings

- Structure and techniques
- Handling people.

Participants can act as a quality circle during the programme or can bring their problems to work on.

The whole team can be trained together, or the team leader can use the training materials to train his team, introducing techniques at appropriate stages, for example:

- Brainstorming at first meeting when establishing ideas to work on or defining the problem fully

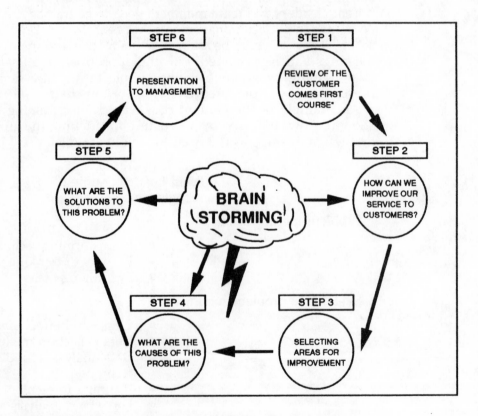

Figure 13.5   VAG (UK)'s programme for training team leaders

- Cause and effect when trying to establish probable causes, with the whole group producing a fishbone diagram to analyse causes
- Presentation skills at the time when the group are ready to prepare their recommendations for management.

Volkswagen Audi Group (UK) used a step-by-step programme for training team leaders in their dealerships as part of their Customer Comes First programme (Figure 13.5). The training programme followed the systematic steps and team leaders were given training materials to take their groups through the same steps whilst addressing real improvement opportunities in the workplace.

BA, Lloyds, VAG (UK), ICI and many others have shown the potential of structured involvement programmes to introduce many more staff to the processes of management and to improve the quality of goods and services provided to customers. As we showed earlier, staff can also become a key part of the ongoing audit and corrective action programme, and can be involved in the development of standards and monitoring mechanisms, which they then own.

However, for every successful involvement programme there are many which have not been successful or whose initial success has not been sustained because management have not given the teams sufficient attention or not helped them build on early success.

14
Keeping up the momentum

As the service campaign progresses, there will need to be constant reinforcement of the Customer First message. Campaigns always tend to flag, and interest has to be regularly re-kindled by further creative programmes.

There are many ways in which the service messages can be reinforced on a continuous basis:

- Celebrate successes, set out new improvement plans, feature customer opinion, and so on using the full range of communication devices at your disposal.
- Build the service philosophy into all company training programmes – induction, technical and business awareness rather than using the more traditional compartmentalized approach.
- Reward those people who most visibly support the service strategy and deliver real improvements in quality and customer service.

Each of these is explored more fully in the rest of this chapter, showing practical ways of using organizational communication media to support the service thrust.

Communication

Company newspapers or newsletters can be used to feature and support the launch and can regularly feature success stories, team projects, customer visits and so on connected with the service programme.

Noticeboards are a source of information for many, as employee audits show, yet they are usually very unprofessionally presented and managed. Develop branded noticeboards featuring service and quality information, performance graphs, team photos and so on. Noticeboards are one of the best ways to show how serious the company is about service improvement. They must be kept up to date, which demands clear ownership, and this is an opportunity to delegate into the work area and generate local pride in achievements.

The service campaign must be effectively and consistently 'marketed'. Merchandising must be in keeping with the culture of the organization and not become gimmicky. The theme and logo can be used, however, as a vehicle to get things done which may not previously have been acceptable. For instance, persuading staff to set service standards which would have been difficult for management to impose. This seems to be one of the hardest aspects for many managers to understand; rather than fighting the campaign, they can actually use it to achieve their own aims, plans and changes.

Where team briefing exists, this must be used in relation to the service campaign. Quality, safety and service performance can be standard items in the core brief and developed in the local briefs on the basis of local achievements. As team briefing is supposed to be two-way communication, these subjects provide ideal material to debate and an opportunity to praise the team for good performance. It also provides a constant stream of data from staff about service and quality performance and initiatives.

Where regular trade union consultation and briefing takes place, quality and service should also be standard items. The philosophy of serving the customer better is one the trade unions generally support. Keep them up to date on the service performance standards the customers expect of their members and where service and quality fit within the overall business goals.

Management must take every opportunity to reinforce the service message. Management presentations should use the terminology of the campaign, constantly emphasizing its importance. Management visibility is part of the concept of recognizing and serving internal customers – after all, staff are the customers of their managers. MBWA is essential, and the importance of quality and service must be reflected in the way managers behave when walking about. Do they overlook poor quality, do they know the team leaders of the involvement programme, do they know what projects are being worked on? The manager concerned about what to talk about when walking about now has a wealth of opportunity provided by the service initiative. Talk about the graph on the wall, ask what improvements are being implemented, what the benefits are of being on the project team, what staff thought of their last event and so on.

Training

Training and education activities should be designed to enable all employees to do their jobs well and fully develop their capabilities. We have seen how training programmes or events specific to the service campaign will differ from traditional training approaches. Traditional programmes which continue in the company must be reviewed and amended so that they support the new values and service focus. The most important to review are:

- *Induction:* one of the 'people systems' referred to earlier. All new starters must understand the service strategy – why quality and service are important to the organization and how they can contribute. New employees will recognize that the company values them, if they are given a professional introduction. Much of the material generated by the service initiative can be re-used, perhaps in a permanent induction room.

  The part played by managers in the induction process starts from the moment a job interview is set up to long after the newcomer starts work. In fact, induction never really stops. People taking up new jobs or promotion need induction to their new roles. Organization changes often leave individual job holders behind, so induction becomes a continuous process, although it may be called something else. BA's A Day in the Life was an induction programme for 40,000 people, many with 25 or more years' service.

- *Technical:* skill and knowledge training. This is often separated from customer relations skills – if the latter is taught at all. Teaching a cashier to operate a till should not be dealt with separately from skills of service. The customer does not have a perception of the job as two separate aspects, but is concerned with the service as a whole.

  'Sitting with Nelly' or 'shadowing' is not always a sufficiently professional way of training. Technical training programmes need to be reconsidered in the context of the total job and the new service emphasis. Technical trainers should at least link their programmes to the service situations in which the technical skills will be used. One of the most important areas is where keyboard operators have to be ready to maintain eye contact and dialogue with the customer while handling the computer transaction. A holistic approach to training is required in such situations. Unfortunately, few technical trainers have an understanding of the total front-line job and how the technical expertise fits into the job as a whole. However, if the need to change is not recognized, training will lose credibility and will undermine the service strategy. 'New look' technical programmes are an essential signal of change.

  Review of systems and procedures will inevitably show the need for more customer-oriented processes, and these will have to be built into training programmes. The reasons for and benefits of such change will have to be explained, and this is an opportunity to emphasize the focus on service. The obsession with putting the customer first – rather than the technical procedure – then starts to penetrate the fabric of the organization and service systems are re-designed in a way which promotes the staff/customer interaction.

- *Quality techniques*: Training in specific quality techniques is worth separating from other technical training if only so that it receives the emphasis it deserves. Good service to the customer depends on quality being built into all elements of the business process – support services as well as production. Training in quality techniques was earlier discussed in the context of staff involvement, and it should be as widespread as possible if everybody is to understand the nature of quality improvement. Crosby, Juran and Deming all propose training for all employees; and Tom Peters gives it overriding emphasis in his book *Thriving on Chaos*. Statistical techniques, data presentation and problem solving are possibilities for some or all of the workforce, supported by a general awareness programme for all. Specially targeted quality training, such as statistical process control or quality assurance systems may also be required.

    There are many commercial sources of quality training, and many technical colleges provide training for industry which can be custom designed to a company's needs. The training needs to be packaged as a coherent whole, supporting the overall service quality theme and using the campaign logo. Training should at all times be presented in a quality manner and setting.

- *Interactive skills:* serving customers, selling skills, interviewing, counselling and appraisal, problem solving and group processing skills – all require a new impetus. The staff awareness programme will be the context and the motivator for front-line staff to acquire better skills in many of these areas. The management programmes will similarly lead to demand by managers for a better understanding of specific skills which can improve performance. To meet demands for better communication, clearer objectives and feedback you will need a menu of training modules. The training department will need to be flexible and energetic in responding to its internal clients' quest for quality and service improvement. Again, there are opportunities to brand much of this training within the overall service initiative.

- *Business awareness:* The staff attitude survey will almost certainly show that many employees lack understanding about other parts of the business and the total context within which they work. Induction programmes are an opportunity to remedy this, but it may well be the longer-serving employees who are most in need. There are a number of ways of increasing employees' knowledge about the rest of the business:
- Visits to customer and supplier departments to find out what their

needs and constraints are and break down the organizational barriers inhibiting change

- Presentation by one department to another, using people across all levels to do the presentations
- A programme on the lines of British Airways' A Day in the Life where the organization presents itself in a structured way to all employees, through exhibitions, presentations, discussions and audio-visual materials
- Customer visits and presentations, showing the importance of listening to customers and understanding their needs
- Job swaps which are well publicized and used as learning opportunities.

All these activities provide an opportunity to involve many staff and build up their pride in themselves, their departments and the enterprise as a whole. New skills are discovered and creativity and innovation abound, which obviously boosts morale and overall performance. The untapped potential of any organization is immense.

Recognition schemes

We are talking here about rewarding those people who improve their performance and demonstrate their commitment to the customer. Reward and feedback reinforce the importance of such performances to the company, provide visible demonstration of management commitment, and motivate people. There are many ways of providing recognition, and a combination appropriate to the organization should be developed:

- Small 'spot' awards presented on a regular basis to people who contribute to improved quality and service in a variety of minor ways. Awards need not be financial. Public recognition and celebration are often adequate reward in themselves.
- Features on improvement ideas, whether from individuals or teams, in company newspapers or in special bulletins, are a useful form of recognition and also play an important role in reinforcement, creating peer pressure to encourage others.
- A company award scheme – with big prizes and/or a sense of occasion – can act as a very important signal. A trophy held for a period of time, lunch with the chief executive, involvement in an external promotional activity, a dinner or a show for award winners and spouses are all ways of celebrating excellence in customer service. Award winners can be nominated by their managers or their peers. Awards should be based on clear criteria, or the scheme will undermine itself. Spot awards can be given on a quota basis, but with the big awards, excellence has to be the watchword, and quotas are not appropriate.

- Although it is culturally difficult for many organizations, basing part of every employee's remuneration on the achievement of service standards is possible once clear standards and credible monitoring systems have been set up. That is, when the organization's commitment to quality of service is unequivocal. If it will take time to implement such a proposal throughout the organization it may be best to start with managers. (See Chapter 15 for how to build this into the management system.) It is also sometimes more appropriate to reward performance, when a team effort can produce results that individuals could not.
- Suggestion schemes are a widely used form of recognition, although most have a poor reputation for management response time and the number of employees who take part. Schemes can be revitalized by the service initiative, providing more opportunities for people to be involved in the implementation of their own ideas. Suggestion schemes are often owned jointly with the trade union, so it may not be appropriate to bring it right under the Customer First umbrella, but link should be created.

15
Managing a service business

In any business the onus is on the managers to point the way and create the right environment for success. This chapter sets out for managers in a service business the principal ways of managing their own performance and that of their department and bringing about change. Employees often look to their manager to set the style, to demonstrate what is important and to decide the pace of work. Nearly all changes which are needed will have to be initiated by management – revolutions rarely happen 'bottom-up'. It is, therefore, worth re-stating at this stage some of the ideas most relevant to effective management in a service business.

Vision

All managers need to understand the corporate vision, mission or objectives and be able to explain them in a way which makes sense to their own people. They should consider working with their team to define departmental missions which are complementary to each other. They should be able to describe the department's main purpose and motivate people in the right direction.

Key results

The work on vision should lead to clarification of the results and targets to be achieved in the coming months. These should be expressed as between five and seven key results, at least two of which should be mainly concerned with quality and customer service. Key results should be about change – improvement, innovation, implementation – not about maintaining status quo. Targets, set in terms of quality, quantity, cost and/or timescale, should provide the milestones and review points.

It is difficult to measure some jobs in this way, but how else can their real worth to the organization be established? Objectives systems designed purely to fill up the annual appraisal report and not used to foster real performance improvement, are a waste of time. A 90-day review system is needed: two hours every three months on each direct report is managerial time well spent. A 90-day review period allows for changes in priority, correction of work which has gone off course, and reallocation of resources. The annual review and report then becomes more meaningful and less traumatic.

If managers are not assessed for their contribution to customer service, then the organization is not really serious about putting the customer first.

Once a key result system is implemented, it is much easier to reward managerial performance. The reward system should reflect and support the service strategy, rather than working against it by encouraging caution and mediocrity.

Exemplifying the new values

Managers will be observed carefully by their subordinates for signals of commitment to Customer First. These are some of the ways in which managers can demonstrate their customer orientation:

- Referring to customers and customer data frequently
- Not accepting poor quality and 'it's near enough' attitudes
- Making direct contact with customers on a regular basis
- Breaking down barriers between departments, rather than protecting their own territory; demonstrating the importance of the internal customer concept.
- Praising people for good performance, particularly where it is overtly supporting the service emphasis
- Being visible in their own department and in customer departments, and taking time to update people on performance successes
- Implementing a 90-day review system for the department
- Encouraging staff to be involved in performance improvement, problem solving and innovation, and showing an interest in team and project activity
- Keeping subjects such as quality, safety and customer high on their own and their department's agenda
- Setting high personal standards in terms of presentation, courtesy and quality and rate of work.

Managers must be careful to avoid sins of omission: not taking the trouble to acknowledge a particularly good piece of work can easily lead people to suspect lack of interest or commitment.

Performance data

Managers who are serious about performance improvement, measure it. 'What gets measured gets done' is a Tom Peters maxim which, put alongside a clear sense of priorities, is very powerful. Individuals and departments should set a handful of work standards which reflect the needs of customers (preferably developed jointly with those customers); by which performance can regularly be measured. The resulting data should be presented creatively and very visibly. Any departments which can't agree performance standards with their customers should consider whether they need to exist at all. Some departments may even find it difficult to decide who their customers are! Using measurement in the key results areas can add meaning to the objectives and help chart progress towards them.

Examples of performance standards are:

- Answering telephones in the sales department
- Accuracy of delivery to the warehouse by the production department, and amount of damage and so on.
- Monthly accounts delivered on time by the accounts department
- Number of bug-free systems from management services department, and projects delivered on time
- Pay systems with no errors
- Point-of-sale material available one week before product launch.

Each standard should reflect a '100 per cent right first time' performance, and any which demand less must be seen as stepping stones towards that goal. This concept has to be interpreted for each department, but the sum of the parts must ultimately be perfect products and services every time.

Accuracy of 98 per cent may sound great to managers who know how difficult it is to achieve, but the fact that 2 per cent of the customers get wrong or damaged orders cannot be justified.

Displaying data is important. It needs to be done simply and attractively. Make sure it is in colour, uses bar charts or graphs rather than columns of numbers, and is branded with the campaign logo. Put it on special noticeboards. Keep it up to date, talk about it with staff when you are on walkabout. Encourage your staff to seek training in simple measurement techniques to support their problem solving. Establish statistical expertise within your department and let people know that help is available.

Finally, use the data as a regular agenda item in your meetings. Have a regular performance meeting to review your performance against service standards. Investigate shortfalls and praise improvements, and ensure that the right people see the data.

Data can be very boring or they can provide you and your department with interest and excitement.

Audit your department

When the campaign starts, announce your own material and personal service audit to demonstrate commitment. Involve people in identifying all the systems, procedures and rules which are unhelpful to the customer and which impede fast response and innovation. Scrap the worst offenders and change the rest. Has the supervisor, for instance, become just the guardian of these inhibiting rules and procedures? Can the role be changed into an enabling one? How effective are your people? Do they understand what's expected of them? Are they capable of delivering it? Could they become so with the right training and other resources? If so, set this up. Stand back from your department and make sure you know:

- Who your customers are
- What they expect of you
- How well you meet those expectations
- What needs to be done to improve
- What are the inhibitors and barriers.

Discuss these questions with all your staff and check your findings with your customers. Make sure you understand the factors critical to their success.

Create action plans for improvement using task forces, champions and so on, and check these plans with your internal and external customers. With the latter group you may feel you are taking a commercial risk, but as they already know your failings, you can only enhance your reputation by showing them that you are aiming to overcome them.

Eradicate the 'manager knows best' attitude; your years of experience may have become your own worst enemy. Establish what factors influence customers' success. Talk to them regularly and use market research selectively and intelligently. Listen to your staff – the experts; find out what they think is wrong and what needs to be done to put it right.

Training

It is the manager's job to ensure that training programmes as outlined in Chapter 14 are put into place for their staff. But managers themselves need training to manage service businesses effectively.

One area in which training programmes may be needed is the management of change:

- Why change is necessary
- The corporate vision and mission
- How to be a change agent

- What are the demands on managers
- Personal assessment
- Personal action planning
- Measuring performance
- Building an effective team
- How to give positive leadership.

Managers need to become comfortable with change, accepting it as part of normal life rather than constantly striving for stability which is impossible. In programmes such as the above managers debate with external facilitators and their colleagues the need for change and the process of change. They then proceed to establish their own roles in that process. Techniques can include vision exercises, domainal mapping, key result generation, peer and subordinate data, action planning and critical success factor analysis. Managers need to understand why people resist change and to learn ways of overcoming the resistance of people who are territorial; who have a high need for structure; who dislike risk; who think in black and white; or who always see the negative aspects rather than the opportunities.

Another area in which training may be required is that of service quality management:

- Creating service excellence
- The marketplace context
- Customer needs and expectations
- Managing the customer experience
- Quality and service principles and techniques
- Standards and monitoring; measurement and charting
- Developing improvement/innovation
- Role modelling
- Developing a service team.

This type of programme concentrates more specifically on customer service and the added value and differentiation it provides in the marketplace. Discussion of customer research and customer success factors leads to an understanding of the principles behind quality and service standards and monitoring mechanisms. Finally there is an opportunity to reinforce messages of the service campaign, and particularly the importance of managers providing a role model for the new corporate values.

Either of the above programmes, or a combination of the two, should play an important role in generating the ownership and commitment of managers across the organization, and should be commenced at an early stage in the campaign.

British Airways developed its first programme for managers, Managing People First, nearly two years into its Customer First programme. Ideally to help managers cope with the attitudinal changes taking place below them, it should have been introduced earlier. The programme content is outlined below and reflects the values and skills identified as germane to effective management in the new British Airways culture.

Managing People First

Leadership Themes:

Urgency, Vision, Motivation, Trust, Taking responsibility

Programme Activities

Self audit
Listening
Key Result Areas
Subordinate/Associate data feed-back
Recognition
Network assessment
Teamwork
Trust Agreements

Follow up

Individual Action Programmes
Support Groups

Performance Management – Personal Review

An organization introducing key result systems to support its service strategy, will need a workshop solely on the aspect of performance management, or personal review to cover:

- Defining key results
- Setting targets
- Appraisal interviewing
- Giving feedback
- Counselling and coaching
- Career management.

These could be approached on a modular basis or in a single programme.

Practice in defining key results for your own and your subordinates' jobs is a good discipline in itself: what are you and your unit supposed to be achieving? Discussions with colleagues in the workshop will help to clarify key result areas – those parts of your job that really count. Targets for change, improvement or innovation can be given deadlines, milestones, standards, success criteria, or measurement methods, as appropriate. These then form the basis for regular review of your key results with your boss, and of your subordinates' key results with you.

Many managers will not have the skills to make such a review system work: skills of appraisal interviewing – giving feedback, jointly setting objectives, handling poor performance; and skills of counselling and coaching – helping people solve problems for themselves and improve key aspects of their job. Meaningful training requirements and realistic career plans which meet both company and individual's needs can therefore arise from the review discussions.

A 'quality' manager in a service business could be said to need the following attributes:

- Total commitment to quality and customer service
- Capable of both strategic and tactical thinking and able to stand back and evaluate the unit's performance
- Able to demonstrate effective customer response by own example
- Able to build warm, friendly relationships based on trust
- Able to recognize and reward good customer service and creative and innovative ideas
- Able to define standards of excellence, observe and give feedback
- Visible concern for and care about people.

16

Marketing customer service

As the service strategy model showed, customers are constantly measuring actual or perceived service against the image you are projecting and the promises you are making. They are also telling other potential customers of their experiences and creating their expectations and prejudices. If customer service really differentiates you from your competitors, you need to tell your customers about it. But if you cannot match your own propaganda, you will not be treated kindly in the marketplace. If you cannot fulfil customer expectations which you have deliberately raised, you will have made a rod for your own back.

Advertising raises customer expectations to a certain level. If the product or service meets those expectations, the market position is strengthened but, at the same time, customers expect even better service next time. ⟩ If services fail to meet expectations, then customers are dissatisfied, particularly when an advertising campaign has promised them something better. Staff morale suffers and economic performance declines. Figure 16.1 shows the pattern of events which follows from satisfying or not satisfying customer expectations.

Before converting an internal service improvement programme to an external promotional campaign, there must be real evidence of success, noticed by both staff and customers, and confirmed by research. The internal and external campaigns can then work in harmony with each other.

There may be three separate external targets for this promotional work, depending on your mission statement. Customers will be the prime target, but suppliers and the community at large may also be important. You can now start briefing suppliers on your requirements as a customer – something you couldn't readily do until your own house had been put in order. Setting clear specifications, delivery dates, technical support and so on enables you to build into contracts, penalties for non-delivery.

There can be useful PR in a quality or service programme which will benefit not only customers but also the community at large – through its greater concern for safety or the environment, for instance. Furthermore,

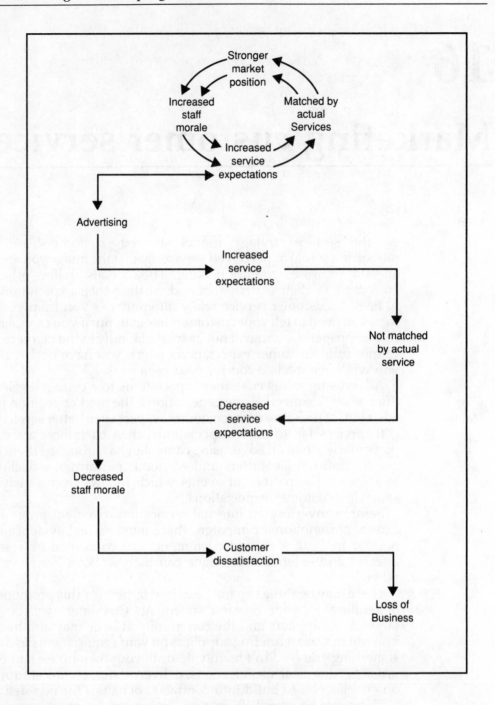

Figure 16.1 Patterns of events when customer expectations are satisfied and dissatisfied

employees who are better trained and more quality-conscious will seek a better quality of life within their community and use their enhanced skills to bring it about. A quality revolution can stretch a long way.

Although the benefits may seem obvious, staff often need to be convinced that the promotion campaign is not a deliberate management ploy to make them work harder. Staff have to see a reason to commit themselves to what is being said to the outside world. If they feel they cannot match the expectations being raised, morale will suffer. One way of getting staff commitment is to involve them in the promotional activities – design and execution. For instance:

- Featuring them in advertisements
- Getting them to contact customers directly about the quality of service
- Ensuring customers are given the name (or names) of staff who serve them, (eg Your room today was cleaned by . . .)
- Asking staff to brief customers about changes to service levels and the rationale behind them
- Fully brief staff on your promotional activities.

There are also a variety of ways of getting customers to notice the difference, in addition to telling them through advertising and promotional messages:

- Set them a challenge to try you out
- Involve them in your advertising
- Get the 'trade' to pass the word around (assuming you have convinced them of the changes)
- Involve customers in agreeing the standards of service you will deliver
- Bring customers into your problem-solving groups – at least they will know you have recognized your weaknesses and are trying to fix them
- Invite them selectively to your training events – as either contributor or participant

It is the noticeable difference which counts. You must be sure it is real and sustainable before communicating it. And you must never become complacent. A competitive edge achieved through improving service can usually be matched quite quickly so use your customer and competitor monitoring to seek new ways of enhancing your lead. You may even be able to use your monitoring activities as a marketing tool to show both confidence and attention to detail.

Figure 16.1 illustrated the importance of meeting expectation in creating repeat business. It costs considerably more to generate new business than it does to keep a loyal, repeat customer. However, few companies invest much sales effort in current customers, and sales targets are often explicitly concerned with new accounts. Customers often feel that interest in them disappears immediately a sale is made. If sales or technical service staff do not offer a consultative, problem-solving approach which is perceived as such by customers, then customer service is not being maximized as a marketing tool.

As consumers are prepared to shop around for suppliers they feel comfortable doing business with, customer service provides a real opportunity to create loyalty. Some obvious tactics to generate more of a partnership feeling with customers are:

- Thank customers for their business, not just at the time of sale but later, as a reminder of your continued interest in their custom; send a card asking for comments about your product and the service given; always thank customers for any referrals
- Keep customers informed of your product or service developments, any awards or commendations received; let them know why you are a better choice than your competitors
- Get involved in customer education; give them ideas on how they can improve their business, not necessarily restricted to the use of your products
- Keep up-to-date lists of your customers, where this is possible. Even the corner shop can keep a list of regulars, their shopping habits, favourite purchases, key dates. This allows you to make small gestures such as a reminder to purchase, or a reminder that a warranty is running out
- Ask your customers' opinion of the way you do business, of improvement ideas, of changes you plan to make. Make your customers feel important and a part of your business – after all you can't exist without them.

The simplest way of marketing customer service is through your customers themselves. Customers will talk about their good and their bad experiences. The more you can do to add value to the products and services you provide, through the ideas outlined above, the more customers will come back and the more referrals you will get from them to colleagues and friends.

17

Handling customer complaints

Your service strategy meets a real test in the way customer complaints are dealt with. As we have said, most customers dissastisfied with your service don't complain – they may put up with it and just grumble to their friends or they may decide to go elsewhere. Complaints, therefore, provide a number of opportunities:

- To identify weaknesses
- To put things right
- To rescue a customer
- To encourage loyalty.

You have to convince everybody in the organization that you should welcome and even seek customer comments and complaints, and that you should handle these consistently and professionally. It should become a natural part of your strategy of listening to customers on a regular basis – complaints form the unsolicited part of the listening process.

If an organization does not feel defensive about complaints, but genuinely sees each one as a learning opportunity, it can actually rescue customers and achieve long-term loyalty. For example, if an airline loses your bag, it creates all sorts of problems for you. If you are asked to fill in a lot of forms, are offered no information on progress and are finally requested to return to the airport to collect your bag, you will not be at all impressed. However, consider the customer-oriented approach:

- Helpful staff taking only the necessary details
- A phone call to your hotel to keep you informed of progress
- Your bag delivered personally by a uniformed member of staff, exactly when promised
- A letter of apology awaiting you on return from your trip.

No complaint will be sent by a customer who is treated in this way. In fact a letter of compliment may be sent and you have a customer for life. The British Airways research showed the importance of rescuing situations – handling delays, diversions, overbookings, food spills and so on in a discreet, honest and professional manner, face to face.

However, when complaints are received, is your organization ready to respond to them and learn from them?

- Where are complaints received?
- Are all managers expected to answer them or is there a central resource?
- How are they logged and progressed?
- Are there clear policies on the key areas of complaint?
- Is there a policy on compensation, replacement, authority levels etc?

Is there a system for dealing with complaints whoever receives them. For example:

- Acknowledgement within 48 hours of receipt
- Request form to appropriate manager for investigation within seven days
- Full reply to the customer with appropriate response within 14 days of receipt
- Each complaint analysed under a number of headings and centrally recorded
- Monthly analysis of numbers and types of complaints produced and widely circulated
- Results of investigation fed to other parts of the organization which can learn from it
- Policy reviewed automatically where investigation shows the complaint has arisen from a process or procedure which is not customer-oriented.

The monthly analysis should be widely circulated to service managers and communicated to front-line staff. It is they who have to respond to the complaints and do things differently in future.

The style of letters has to be thought about – it is easy to be patronizing, or imply that the customer is to blame or to send a standard word-processed reply. Being customer-oriented means scrapping standard paragraphs and answering every letter in an individual way. Certainly there are legal aspects to be considered, but this should not become an excuse for not answering the complaint in the letter. That only results in an even angrier letter from the customer.

If a complaint is handled well there may be no need for compensation, even if this was originally demanded. A sensitively written letter may be able to offer instead a discount on future purchases – at least retaining the customer's business. A badly worded response containing such an offer could, on the other hand, cause more anger.

Where compensation claims are expected and have to be met, guidelines must be clearly set out. This should not, however, restrict managers and staff from using their commonsense – taking risks if necessary – to try and retain a customer's business.

All of this is easier with a specialist department handling customer complaints. Such a unit can also handle personal visits and telephone calls, and it can actively seek reactions from customers – for instance, by calling them after a stay in a hotel, or after hiring a car service to ask them how satisfied they were.

A central department can, however, be perceived by line managers dealing direct with customers to be taking responsibilities and interest away from them. This need not be so. They will be involved in the investigation process; they may be the best people to follow-up with the customer once the complaint has been investigated. They should get copies of the letters which concern their areas, should be involved in deciding compensation policy and corrective action. Finally, they should be expected to respond to the monthly complaints analysis giving clear action plans on the areas highlighted.

One further way of using customer complaints to heighten customer awareness is to use their content:

- In staff training programmes concerning more difficult customer relations
- As a regular feature in the staff newspaper
- By having mail opening sessions in senior and staff meetings (making sure the letters are not lost in the process, of course). Opening the day's complaints and sharing them in a group can be useful warning against complacency.

Complaints should not be avoided – there are bound to be customers dissatisfied with some aspects of your service, and you need to know about them. Any customer who takes the trouble to write to you deserves a thoughtful response from you. Using the service strategy model you can decide where the fault lies:

- in poor product quality
- in a delivery system not customer-oriented
- in a staff attitude problem
- in image projection creating too high an expectation.

In fact, customer complaints can be used as an integral part of your staff involvement activity. They provide a regular supply of issues that have to be looked at and put right.

Some of your complaints are bound to be bogus – customers wanting something for nothing, people who always complain. But it's better to accept the occasional abuse of your system than to suspect all complainants of trying to con you. Marks & Spencer have a policy of replacement without argument. Obviously they sometimes have to replace goods which are old not faulty, but the cost of this must be far outweighed by the competitive benefit provided by this policy.

Once you have an organization comfortable with handling customer complaints you can actively seek customer comment. Comment cards are often seen in hotels. Other more imaginative approaches are:

- To display your customer charter and invite comment whenever you fall short of what you are offering to deliver
- To set up informal discussion groups with your customers and be prepared to listen, not react defensively; ask for their help in improving your service. Offer an incentive to attend if you think that would be appropriate
- To ask staff to talk to a specific number of customers per period to see what aspects of their service could be improved; use your staff to assess and implement these improvements.
- To invite customers to record their views on a service they have just received by using a video box such as that installed at Heathrow by BA.

The complaints system

As we mentioned earlier, all complaints must be handled systematically. One possible system is set out below, followed by some guidelines for its use.

1. Log the complaint (preferably on a form such as that shown in Figure 17.1):
    - Who received it
    - How it was received (telephone, letter, direct)
    - Nature of complaint (full description)
    - Date/time of complaint (so you can meet your stated performance standard)
    - Any interim 'fix-it' action required.

2. Inform customer you are dealing with the complaint, the likely timescale and any immediate action taken.

3. If you are not the person who can solve the problem, send a copy of the details to the person who can. (If interim action has been required you will probably have already spoken to them.)

4. Note any action taken at the time of the complaint to attempt to solve the problem.

5. Once the problem has been resolved complete notes of action taken.

6. Write/speak to the customer to tell them what action has been taken.

   - To solve their problem
   - To resolve any underlying causes of their problem
   - To provide compensation.

7. Send the person who received the complaint a copy of the form showing the action taken and, where appropriate, a copy of the letter to the customer.

8. Ensure the complaint has been analysed and fed into a central data system. No matter how small the organization, keeping a record of complaints is worthwhile so that trends can be identified.

Complaints may be received by a number of people and departments in the organization. Many will need guidelines on the style of answering complaints as well as understanding the need for a systematic approach.
   Useful hints are:

1. If the customer is speaking to you direct:

   - Listen carefully
   - Don't interrupt or argue
   - Get the facts
   - Act assertively, not aggressively or submissively
   - Don't take it personally.

2. On the basis of the facts:

   - Decide whether you can take action or whether you need to refer it
   - Agree action with the customer or advise them of your intention and reasons for referring it
   - Give clear timescales of action.

3. Keep the customer advised at all times of progress

4. Implement action, but always double check that what you wanted to happen has happened.

5. Confirm the outcome with the customer; use the opportunity to try and repair a business relationship for the future.

Acknowledgement sent .... Date .... Target for ....
full response

Customer Complaint Progress record	Name of Customer
	Address
How received?	
Letter Ref:	
Telephone	Contact tel no.
Face to face	
Who received complaint	Date/time complaint type (code)

Nature of complaint

Figure 17.1   Complaint record

Immediate action taken/referred to

Action taken	Who by	Date

Confirmation sent to customer   Date   Reference

Reason for delay from target

Figure 17.1   Complaint record concluded

6.   Take any necessary action to avoid it happening again, including informing all those who need to know, explain clearly the problem dealt with and the solution offered to remove the root cause.

7.   Remember that a complaint is an opportunity and a second chance not offered by most dissatisfied customers. Complaints are a constant source of ideas for improving customer service.

Summary of Part II

To develop an effective service improvement programme:

- The organization needs a stated common sense of purpose.
- Ownership has to be widespread; a champion may be needed to inject energy and to co-ordinate.
- The organization needs a continuous stream of data from customer surveys, internal audits and quality assurance activities to drive and monitor the programme.
- A long-term programme is required, starting with at least a two-year plan of activities.
- Activities have to be branded to aid coherence and marketing of the message.
- People change systems not vice versa: awareness and commitment programmes can create a climate in which people want to change the systems.
- Improvement projects should involve as many people as possible, trained to analyse problems and remove root causes, building quality into the improved processes.
- Communication and training activities must be re-appraised to ensure they support the new emphasis on customer service.
- Quality improvement has to be managed, largely by managers; managing the status quo is not acceptable.
- Service can be a powerful marketing tool – when the time is right – to add value and provide a competitive edge.
- A complaints system is essential (and may be mandatory under some QA systems) to make sure that opportunities to improve are properly taken.
- Quality improvement requires a substantial commitment and must be an integral part of the managerial process.

Part III
The British Airways story

Introduction

In setting out to establish greater customer orientation in your organization, it is well worthwhile looking at the experience of others who have succeeded in this quest. Most of the organizations which have been referred to previously in this book have been inspired by the pioneering work carried out by British Airways. The author was closely involved in producing the remarkable culture change at BA, and the final part of this book tells the story of that change. Lessons are drawn from BA's experience and links are made to the service strategy model which was in fact developed partly on the basis of the BA improvement programmes.

British Airways did not have the best of starting points – huge losses, redundancies and a poor service image; yet the optimists, including Colin Marshall, recognized that performance could only go in one direction – upwards. Putting the customer first was seen both as the route and the rallying call. Following detailed customer and staff research, the strategic direction was set and Customer First was launched.

Objectives and success criteria were defined, albeit crudely, and service improvement activities set in motion. These included an awareness programme for all staff, communication of customer-led service standards, performance management mechanisms and service improvement teams, all branded and presented under the Customer First umbrella.

The long-term nature of the campaign meant that a follow-up staff programme was needed to broaden understanding of the total business. This created a well informed section of staff who could take collective responsibility for improving service. The improved level of knowledge among staff was also very useful in the build up to flotation. Many senior and middle managers felt uneasy about the new values of quality and service which seemed to threaten old values of professionalism and hierarchy. Managing People First was a programme designed to help managers themselves with the transition and to enable them to manage their subordinates through the transition. An important learning point for other organizations is not to leave such an intervention until it is too late. Managers manage performance improvement and need help to do so.

The final stage of the story is about how BA held the gains by continuing to capture data and use it creatively: by creating a third staff event exploring and explaining the competitive context; by follow-up management training looking at leadership within a service business; and by a whole range of other communication and training activities designed to keep Customer First well and truly alive in the organization.

18

The background

In 1974 British European Airways and British Overseas Airways Corporation merged, with the aim, as British Airways, of creating economies of scale and a worldwide network and reputation. By the late 1970s, few economies of scale had been achieved and the airline had nearly 60,000 staff. It was decided to take advantage of substantial market growth by handling a larger business with the same size staff. Unfortunately, following the Middle East oil crisis, the market decreased, and 1979 brought a decision to reduce to a figure of 35,000 staff. Comparative studies showed that this could represent a lean and competitive airline.

A Corporate Employment Strategy, consisting of a suite of policies, was put together to facilitate the run down and retrenchment. It included dealing with route and station closures, severance and redeployment, and the rules for carrying these out. Over the following three years, staff numbers were reduced to 37,500. Momentum was created by some tough targets and timescales set by the Chairman, Lord King, and the trade unions gave their support in principle. The three years were known as the 'survival period' – a traumatic but necessary part of the history of the airline.

Following this period, which also included huge financial losses, morale was at its lowest, with many thinking that those who had left had got the best deal. Many people were in jobs they did not want to be in, with inadequate skills; everybody had tighter rosters and routines, less overtime and generally more work. However, BA was fitter and leaner and ready to take advantage of a reviving marketplace.

The marketplace was characterized by increasing competition through deregulation. The airline world in general operates in a difficult economic, geographical and political environment, which is constantly changing. Consumerism was growing, with passengers demanding more and less prepared to accept mediocrity.

In February 1983 a new Chief Executive, Colin Marshall, was appointed. His experience with Avis and Sears Holding led him to the view that British Airways had to be made to reflect the needs of the marketplace. Material aspects of the service certainly required improvement, but the main difference would depend on personal aspects of the service being upgraded to create a real competitive edge. Marshall appointed a four-man team, called the Marketing Policy Group, to identify the broad areas where change was needed and action plans were put in place. A set of corporate objectives (shown below) were communicated throughout the organization; service stands out as the key element.

Corporate objectives

1. To provide the *highest levels of service* to all customers, passengers, shippers, travel agents and freight agents.
2. To preserve high professional and technical standards in order to achieve the highest levels of safety.
3. To provide a *uniform image worldwide* and to maintain a *specific set of standards* for each clearly defined market segment.
4. *To respond quickly and sensitively to the changing needs of our present and potential customers.*
5. To maintain and, where opportunity occurs, expand our present route structure.
6. To manage, operate and market the airline in the most efficient manner.
7. *To create a service and people oriented work environment*, assuring all employees of fair pay and working conditions and continuing concern for their careers.

These objectives presented Marshall's philosophy of service as the central strategic value and were widely communicated. The message to managers was loud and clear: a service emphasis would not reduce professionalism and efficiency, but would add value to those areas where there had already been hard earned gains.

Change issues

Organisation

Aircraft and crew availability, scheduling rules and pooling agreements dominated BA decisions about how to serve the marketplace. The bureaucratic culture took little account of the consumer's perception of its product. This was a condition which called for major surgery, and in July 1983 the organization was changed virtually overnight, with the loss of some 70 senior managers. Marketing strength was built up to define the market and influence demands which would be delivered by the Operations Department. In addition to the usual service departments (Finance, Personnel, Computing and so on), a new department was created, called

Marketplace Performance. With the role of ombudsman, internal critic and champion of the customer, this small unit was established to ensure the market orientation concept worked in practice.

The philosophy behind the organizational change, the new units and the individual management jobs, were set out in two comprehensive booklets prepared by Colin Marshall, an external consultant, and the members of the Marketing Policy Group, Unusually for BA at the time, and since, the process of planning organizational change was a well kept secret until the day of announcement.

External image

The second area of change required was in the way the airline projected and promoted itself to the outside world. Research had shown a poor service reputation and the previous year a policy decision had been taken to remove service claims from advertising. Research had also shown that BA was not known internationally as well as BOAC had been. The emphasis was, therefore, shifted to the size and international stature of the company.

A strong statement on external image was needed. The two main areas where image counts in the airline world are the company's livery and the uniforms of the customer contact staff. The search was started for a new livery and new uniform early in 1983, but it was 1987 before these parts of the programme of change had been completed. Amidst some controversy, a non-UK company – Landor from San Francisco – was chosen to create a new livery for aircraft, sales shops, stationery and all merchandizing materials – a substantial task. The result reflected the best traditions of the airline and the new excitement. It was generally well received with an impressive launch for external opinion formers and some 10,000 staff, who received a big boost to morale.

Staff uniform development was a longer process with a number of designers considered and a full consultation programme organized for staff. The search was for a uniform which would convey both sophistication and friendliness.

Attitude change

It was quickly understood that changing the external face of BA would have little impact unless internal attitudes also changed to support the new customer orientation. The prevalent 'manager knows best' behaviour which dominated could not continue, and the staff behaviour perceived by the customers to be – at best – professional but cold and aloof had to change. Before an attitude change programme could be devised, BA needed to know much more about customers' expectations of an airline and their perception of BA's service. The importance of service to the customer in the eyes of BA employees also had to be researched.

A survey was carried out among some 700 air travellers, using a telephone interviewing technique to establish their expectations as

Table 18.1   Summary of BA customer survey

AIRLINE SERVICE – CUSTOMER EXPECTATIONS JUNE 1983

Whom we asked	An independent market research company interviewed 691 recent airline passengers, about half of whom had flown British Airways on their last trip. This was the start of a process by which we will continue to monitor customer views and expectations.
Air travel in general	The research told us clearly that it is experiences passengers have with *staff* which play the major part in generating goodwill. When asked to describe their best experience with an airline, 61 per cent of passengers mentioned a staff factor (eg friendly, efficient, helpful) and 39 per cent described other factors (eg operational, food, seating).
	The importance of staff factors was even further emphasized when passengers were asked to describe their worst experience with an airline. In this situation, 70 per cent mentioned a staff factor compared with 30 percent who mentioned other factors.
	These results highlight the fact that passengers take factors like safety, punctuality, food and cleanliness for granted, and that they differentiate between airlines on staff performance. This provides us with the opportunity to become the best.
Overall view of British Airways	Those interviewed were asked how British Airways staff service compared with 'other international airlines'. In the four areas surveyed (bookings and enquiries, check-in and boarding, in-flight and disembarkation) the most popular answer was that British Airways was 'about the same' as other international airlines. Of those expressing a positive or negative opinion, we were usually seen as being better than the rest, but we must not lose sight of the fact that there was sometimes a substantial minority saying we were worse than the competition.
	These results show that there is a great opportunity for British Airways to improve in the passenger contact area. With just a little effort we can lift ourselves out of the 'all the same' category and make British Airways different from, and therefore better than, all the other carriers.

AIRLINE SERVICE – HOW TO GAIN GOODWILL

Each stage of the journey, from booking through to baggage retrieval, is important to customer satisfaction. Passengers view air travel as a total experience, and not just a flight from A to B. The research highlighted five main areas where we might gain goodwill, on the assumption that if we have their goodwill, we have their business.

Making the best of the occasional bad experience	– Passengers recognize that delays and disruptions are occasionally unavoidable in airline travel, and these situations give us a tremendous opportunity to 'shine' and to regain goodwill. The ability to recover well is of utmost importance.
Showing care and concern	– Customers gain vicarious pleasure from seeing special passengers given individual care and concern. Singling out the elderly, the disabled, families or small children, for personal attention, creates a good impression with all passengers.
Being spontaneous	– Customers enjoy seeing staff adding a personal touch to the standard systems and procedures. Initiating non-routine interactions, and even going beyond the rule book, add to this feeling.
Recognizing and handling anxieties	– Many passengers experience concern and anxiety, and they appreciate help and reassurance when necessary.
Anticipating problems and initiating solutions	– Goodwill can be gained by anticipating a customer's problems, and by proposing solutions. Their goodwill is generated by being pro-active, and not merely waiting for the customer to present us with his problem.

customers, both on the ground and in the air. The research sought to discover where customer goodwill could be generated, on the assumption that goodwill was a key factor in creating repeat business. A summary of the research is shown in Table 18.1. Interviewees were asked first for general views of air travel and then opinions of how BA measured up against criteria they felt were important. Some two-thirds stated that BA was neither better nor worse than other airlines. While this was not good news for 'the world's favourite airline' it actually showed the enormous potential for BA to create a real competitive edge through a better all-round quality of service.

The research showed that giving information, solving problems of missed connections, handling check-in queries, being alert to anxiety, all provide the 'individualization' valued so highly by the customer. As the analysis of service anecdotes in Chapter 9 also showed, giving better information and/or taking anticipatory action can compensate for poor service and result in retaining customers.

A staff attitude survey was also carried out by Fay Fransella of the Centre for Personal Construct Psychology, using the repertory grid technique of construct analysis. This clearly showed that professionalism (which to them meant they were doing their job technically well) and sociability (towards themselves and to customers prepared to be sociable with them), were the two most important values held by staff. Satisfying the needs of individual customers, with different and sometimes difficult requirements, featured well down their priority lists, perhaps reflecting the values expressed by the organization towards them during the previous few years.

Managers saw service as being important, but few saw it as the most crucial part of doing a good job. Financial and operational targets still dominated, again reflecting the focus of the previous years. Most supervisors felt badly treated by the organization as a whole, and saw themselves not as agents of change, but as guardians of the rule book. Very few of the rules supported the new customer orientation.

In essence, the organization had worked hard to standardize front-line interaction with the customers and service routines. But research was now showing that neither passengers nor staff wanted this to continue. It also revealed the gap between what customers wanted and what staff in general thought they should be delivering. The challenge was to motivate staff to take responsibility for the service outcome and achieve satisfaction from handling the 'moments of truth' to suit the needs of the individual customer and their own professionalism. An internal attitude change programme was therefore launched in autumn 1983, called 'Putting the Customer First'.

19
The customer first campaign

A logo representing a caring relationship between staff and the customer supported the slogan 'Putting the customer first'. Together they described a state of mind required by all employees of British Airways. Success criteria for the campaign were agreed, which could be measured as the campaign progressed. Financial business targets were not set, although it was clear that some £2 million per annum would need to be spent on this programme of activities and that commercial benefits were expected to result from such an investment. The success criteria were:

- In terms of the customer:
  - All staff are convinced of the need to 'put the customer first'.
  - Research-based customer service standards are established and communicated to the staff who have to work to them.
  - Effective customer monitoring is established.
  - Data are produced which show that customer satisfaction has increased as a result of the campaign.

- In terms of the staff:
  - All staff feel that management mean business.
  - Staff feel they are involved practically in defining and meeting customer needs.
  - Effective staff performance monitoring against customer service standards is established.
  - Staff complaints and suggestions are seen by staff to be effectively followed up.

These are areas which were identified as important by customers and staff. We should return to these later to assess the progress made by BA over a five or six-year period of 'putting the customer first'.

The campaign was presented initially as a four-part approach, supported by a full communication programme (Figure 19.1). Each activity is described in some detail before commenting on how the activities were designed to be mutually supportive. The diagram shows the interrelationships between the activities, so that attendance on the two-day event triggers an interest in joining a Customer First team and the style of the event influences the style of future training. The communication programme was designed to present the activities as an integrated 'branded' whole. Marketing techniques were being used for the first time in a campaign primarily targeted at employees.

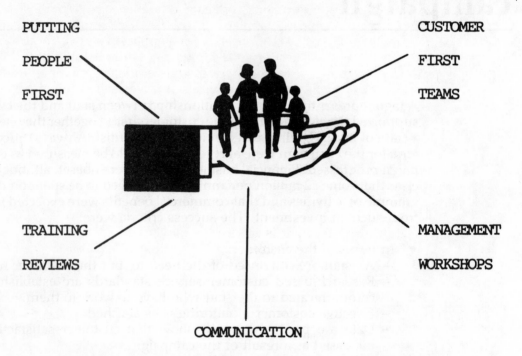

PUTTING PEOPLE FIRST

CUSTOMER FIRST TEAMS

TRAINING REVIEWS

MANAGEMENT WORKSHOPS

COMMUNICATION

Figure 19.1   Putting the customer first: the initial programme structure

Each element of the campaign is now described in detail.

Putting people first (PPF)

In terms of the framework developed in Chapter 13, Putting People First was the first step in a staff awareness programme. A preview given to managers was an early step towards management commitment. Senior managers were also briefed on the total programme by Colin Marshall. Putting People First was initially designed for the 15,000 staff in direct contact with the customer. It was subsequently extended to all staff in the airline, in formats appropriate to different disciplines. The initial programme concentrated on service to the customer and customer expectations reflected in the research. It also explored a whole range of personal development issues, designed to show that after the survival period, individual contributions really would matter. The programme was run by Time Manager International and was conducted in the UK and in some overseas locations. Staff were mixed together from the various disciplines within the airline which proved to be an effective way of getting people to talk through mutual problems in small cross-departmental groups and learn from trainer input and from each other. The programme lasted two days and was run for groups of up to 180, a new and exciting style of training event for BA and necessary for a critical mass to be built quickly.

Not everybody liked Putting People First, either because of the type of messages or the perceived American style of the programme, or because personal experiences in the previous few years had left them feeling disenchanted. Incidentally, much of the programme content originated in Scandinavia, the presenters were British and when the events were presented in New York they were extremely well received. Eventually the programmes ran in Europe, South Africa, Australia and the Indian sub-continent. They provided a very useful basis for the other campaign activities to build upon.

The topics covered by the course and its workbook were:

- Introduction: what is service?
  - Key service examples

- What sort of person would you like to be?
  - Winners and losers
  - I own the problem

- Determining your aims in life
  - What do you want from life?

- Your brain
  - How your brain functions
  - How to make best use of its enormous potential

- Strokes (attention)
  - The importance of attention
  - Types of strokes
  - Giving and receiving strokes

- Choosing how you feel
  - Realistic and unrealistic beliefs
  - How to prevent negative feelings

- Stress
  - The concept of stress
  - How to control stress

- Non-verbal communication
  - Body language
  - Rapport and pacing

- Being assertive
  - Assertive, aggressive or submissive?
  - How to deal with aggressive people

- A positive attitude to life
  - Positive versus negative thinking
  - Service attitude
  - Time in relation to service
  - The first four minutes.

It was for reasons of expediency that the programme covered customer contact staff first. But there were accusations of elitism made by support staff, and a one-day version of PPF was therefore designed for all support staff (Engineering, Information Management, Ground Support, Finance and Helicopters). An additional second day was then designed for each of these areas, involving line management in design and delivery, in order to put the service message into a support context. These 'second day' programmes promoted a much more visible management style throughout these areas.

Putting People First programmes were closed by Colin Marshall himself or by one of his executive team. This made an important statement about the level of commitment by the senior team and provided opportunities for reinforcement and topical updates.

Customer first teams

These teams formed a very practical part of the Customer First programme, far exceeding initial expectations. They were designed on similar lines to quality circles, but they looked out towards the customer interface, not in towards production matters. The teams consisted of staff volunteers and provided a practical way for staff to become involved in improving customer service. Team leaders (usually supervisors) were trained in skills such as brainstorming, problem analysis, group processes and presentation techniques, and they then trained team members as the regular meetings took place. Because of the variety of work patterns in the airline, a flexible approach had to be taken in terms of group size, and length and frequency of meetings. Within a few months, however, around 150 teams had been established worldwide and many hundreds of ideas had been developed and implemented by them.

Each team had access to a trained management facilitator who ensured that they addressed realistic projects, got access to information required and were provided with appropriate facilities. It was also the facilitator's responsibility to ensure that groups worked effectively and that their recommendations were professionally dealt with by the management team.

The benefits have been two-fold. Customers have observed service improvements, and staff have experienced personal development from their team sessions. Once Customer First teams were working successfully a newsletter was launched so that teams could see their work featured, learn about other teams and gain some useful PR. Experience sharing sessions between leaders were set up, and once teams had matured, some cross departmental projects were handled by more than one team working together. Customer First teams have become a very powerful part of the programme which has endured for over three years and involved well over 2,000 staff directly, and many more indirectly through the work of their colleagues. In terms of the service improvement programme, mapped out in Part II, Customer First teams are an excellent example of involving staff in continuous improvement of both material and personal aspects of service.

Management workshops

Although managers were attending PPF, a mechanism was needed to put responsibility for service improvement firmly on the shoulders of line managers – not on the central Customer Service Department – and to generate their commitment and ownership. In all the customer contact units – Cabin Services, Reservations, Passenger Handling and so on – a Management Workshop was set up, chaired by a senior manager in that unit. The aims of the Workshops were to:

- Co-ordinate campaign activities in their area
  - Supporting PPF
  - Co-ordinating Customer First teams
  - Communicating successes
- Set the style and establish role models
- Define customer service standards
- Monitor performance.

The workshops were each asked to convert the customer expectations revealed by the research into a set of delivery statements for their part of the service package. These were all collected in a common style and the

127

What the customer expects

Passengers with special needs, i.e. the old, the young or the infirm need extra care and consideration

Passengers expect a fully professional and personal service

How can we satisfy expectations

— help should be offered to old people, particularly those who experience difficulty in moving. Wherever possible they should be settled into their seats and offered a blanket.

— old people may also experience difficulty in sleeping. Special and frequent efforts should be made during long flights to help pass the time. e.g. old people like to chat especially about relations and the offer of a cup of tea works wonders to cheer them up.

— infirm people have special needs. A personal briefing on toilet facilities will help relieve anxiety. Wherever possible, the offer of help to and from the toilets is much appreciated.

— unaccompanied young people and infirm passengers should never be allowed to feel neglected or abandoned between the cabin crew and the ground staff.

— the offering of drinks, meals, amenities, etc should be undertaken professionally, and courteously. This includes the clearing of debris which should be undertaken promptly and regularly. These contacts also give several opportunities for spontaneous conversation, e.g. 'did you enjoy the film?, did you enjoy your meal?, how was your steak?.' etc.

— where the call bell is used, it should be answered promptly. The request should be met as quickly as possible.

— passengers should never have to ask twice for the same thing. During crew handover all existing undertakings, requests, problems, etc. should be made known to the joining crew so that passenger care continues without involving the passenger in restating his needs.

— passengers should never be given the impression that laid down routines and procedures are more important than the people they serve.

Figure 19.2 Cabin crew standards of service

airline's personal service standards were established for the first time and in a comprehensive, customer-led manner. No matter how imperfect, they provided a great leap forward.

To avoid being just an interesting intellectual exercise, these standards needed to be communicated creatively to the staff who had to achieve them. One example of how the Cabin Services Workshop did this for cabin crew is illustrated in Figure 19.2.

Other parts of the organization took different approaches. As our service strategy model showed, standards based on customer data become a powerful part of the move towards customer focus and continued improvement.

In British Airways the standards were used to dictate training content and as a basis for individual performance assessment by supervisors. As more and more data came in (see 'Monitoring' below), the management workshops evolved to become performance meetings which monitored the service performance of their unit and generated corrective or reinforcement action as appropriate.

Training review

It was essential for the new service orientation to be carried through from PPF to other training activities. All training programmes were reviewed, as were recruitment and selection criteria, to ensure the airline would have staff capable of, and willing to, meet the needs of customers. Initial training programmes were turned on their heads to ensure the customer focus was absolutely clear. Previous training approaches had created the type of standard processing which customers and staff said they disliked. The new approach put the emphasis on the individual customer; and the new training was flexible and based on self discovery.

Some supervisory training programmes were established to support the new approach, but in general, both supervisory and management training were neglected during the early stages of the Customer First programme.

Communication

The campaign was promoted fully through the internal newspaper, *British Airways News*, backed up corporately by the Customer First newsletter, and locally by special bulletins and in-house magazines. A video summarizing the purpose and progress of Customer First after a year or so was widely circulated. Every opportunity was taken to convey the Customer First theme to staff, as only constant reinforcement will ensure that 'putting the customer first' becomes a state of mind. Management speeches, articles, noticeboards and so on were all used creatively to keep the message alive.

129

Material changes

The emphasis of the Customer First initiative was very much on the personal/attitudinal aspects of service, but as our earlier model showed, service comprises both material and personal elements in varying mixes. It was the personal aspects which were most criticised by BA's customers, but the company's service strategy had to cover ways of improving products, environment and delivery systems as well as attitudes, skills and behaviour. This meant attending to many little things which had been neglected during the survival period. Aircraft interiors were given special attention by a manager whose responsibilities crossed traditional boundaries. Customer service computer systems were overhauled to provide staff- and customer-oriented facilities – 'user friendly' check-in for instance. New in-flight equipment was provided – trolleys and ovens that worked without the need for creative genius or brute force.

In-flight entertainment – equipment and content – was brought up to date. 'Squawk' boxes connecting check-in desks to departure gates were fixed, enabling late check-in passengers (aptly called 'have a go!') to get to their aircraft. Radio equipment for staff on the tarmac was uprated for faster communication. Baggage expeditor staff were introduced to gain an extra few minutes for transfer baggage. Leaflets were produced to help elderly or disabled passengers, or those travelling with children, to understand better how to organize their travel – a direct response to the survey findings. Customer First teams looked into specific areas requiring improvement and came up with new working procedures, redesigned lounges and passenger flows, new product packaging (for instance for 'young flyers' – previously known as 'unaccompanied minors'), new equipment for aircraft cleaning, security and baggage. A technology transfer exercise was launched in the areas of baggage loading, catering and cleaning and much was learnt from companies in totally different industries and environments which had addressed similar problems.

Effort continues to be put into material aspects of service such as in-flight product, seating, new aircraft, refurbishment, improved airport facilities and user-friendly systems. The search is for continuous improvements and leading edge innovations, and BA remains constantly alert to the changing needs of an increasingly sophisticated travelling public.

Monitoring

As the strategy model shows, the results of all this effort have to be monitored or measured to keep data flowing into the management system, removing complacency and generating a desire to seek better ways of running the business. The service standards dictate the key areas to monitor, as they are the areas identified by customers as critical to success. In Chapter 13 the standards set for ground service were used to illustrate the monitoring process.

There were a number of areas where monitoring activities were established by BA in the early months:

- *Customer monitor:* Market research continues to play an important part and customers (some 150,000 per year) are interviewed in London, both on arrival and on departure. They are questioned about their satisfaction with service standards on the ground and in the air. Strengths and weaknesses can be identified and new service improvements initiated by the Management Workshops. A 'quick fire' reporting system allows interviewers to respond to a customer's deep dissatisfaction or high praise by generating appropriate rescue or thank-you action.

- *Complaints analysis:* All complaints and compliments are responded to individually by staff in Customer Relations, and each letter (or phone call) is categorized to produce a monthly analysis of complaints. These are also communicated to the Management Workshops as further data to assess performance.

- *Duty travel:* When travelling on duty, managers and staff are asked to complete a questionnaire, commenting not on how *they* were treated, but on how other passengers, whose expectations tend to be different from their own, were treated. A steady trickle of useful data is provided in this way, and there is also an educational benefit from managers and staff viewing the service package through the eyes of the customers.

- *Quality audit:* Although the campaign was directed at the previously neglected area of personal service, there was a need to monitor the material and personal service given in each area. A series of quality audits required managers to obtain performance data against a whole range of service elements, such as queueing, transaction times, telephone answering, baggage delivery and punctuality, in addition to checking good housekeeping, environmental aspects and, of course, personal service. These audits are reviewed quarterly, particularly from all overseas areas. Quality auditing is now the remit of a new department consisting of Senior Quality Executives, showing the close link between launching a service initiative and developing total quality management.

- *Performance indicators (PI):* Marketplace performance, the department independent of both Marketing and Operations, carries out its own quality audit, presenting data and charts (PI), each month to the Chief

Executive and his team. A commentary is provided on trends perceived and, from time to time, a study is included on a key competitor to see where BA is outperforming and where extra effort is needed.

The effect of the campaign has, of course, to be measured in terms of the bottom line. During the first three years of the Customer First campaign, British Airways became profitable and its growth outstripped the market growth. The improvement in performance and in warmth and friendliness had been noticed by customers. Assessment of the campaign's success is provided at the end of Part III. In autumn 1985, the decision was taken on the strength of customer research, to return to advertising based on service promises. Rather than join the many airlines advertising the relationship between pretty girls and male customers, a tongue-in-cheek approach, devised with Saatchi & Saatchi, resulted in the Supercare campaign, featuring staff as superheroes on the lines of Superman and Superwoman. Loved or hated, it certainly got talked about and got the message over that BA was back as a service force.

20

The second phase

After some months of PPF, issues were being raised all over the airline about management style and ability to manage culture change. It was recognized that management initiate and manage change if motivated to do so, otherwise they manage the status quo. They set the tone for customer service by the way they handle their social interactions with staff and the commitment they themselves demonstrate towards service values. In 1985, therefore, a training programme was launched to educate over 1000 managers in better management practice, and to link this more effectively with performance appraisal. At the same time, the intention to introduce a measure of performance-based pay was announced. Research was carried out to establish a list of management practices which, it was felt, would contribute to BA achieving its corporate goals. These practices then underpinned each of the three management change initiatives launched.

Managing people first

This one-week training programme was designed to enable managers from every part of the airline to define their vision for the future, develop a mission for their work units and establish their 'key result areas' which would subsequently drive performance improvement and, as a result, the performance assessment system. In addition, topics such as trust, listening and giving recognition were discussed. The centrepiece of the course, however, was receiving feedback on how each manager measured up to the best practice list.

Questionnaires were given to the manager who handed them out to five subordinates and five peers. After being analysed, the data were fed back to the manager during the course. Whilst some denial of the data took place, the exercise did focus attention on those practices which needed to be improved. A tactics booklet was produced to show how each of the areas could be improved by some commonsense changes to the way a person managed.

The outline programme was presented in the previous section. It was designed to gain management commitment to the service strategy and provide participants with the means to manage the changes required. BA recognized that it should have started this commitment programme much earlier – a lesson for other organizations embarking on the same course.

As a result of the work on vision and mission in the early courses, new mission and goals statements for the 1990s were developed to take the place of the corporate objectives produced some three years earlier. These are set out here and, although a little verbose, show well the changed company style achieved over the three-year period, since the inception of the service philosophy.

The British Airways Mission – to 1990 and beyond
British Airways will have a corporate charisma such that everyone working for it will take pride in the company and see themselves as representing a highly successful worldwide organization.

BA will be a creative enterprise, caring about its people and its customers.

We will develop the kind of business capability which will make BA the envy of its competitors, to the enhancement of its stakeholders.

British Airways will be a formidable contender in all the fields it enters, as well as demonstrating a resourceful and flexible ability to earn high profits wherever it chooses to focus.

We will be seen as THE training ground for talented people in the field of service industries.

Whether in transport or in any of the travel or tourism activity areas, the term 'BA' will be the ultimate symbol of creativity, value, service and quality.

Management performance appraisal

Task achievement and managerial process skill were assessed equally in the new appraisal system, which was piloted fully before being linked to performance pay. Key results have to be agreed in a two-way discussion with the immediate superior, and these have to be assessed in the annual appraisal. A 90-day review system was encouraged so that data was live and performance frequently discussed and not left as a sterile, annual exercise. In addition to task, managers were rated by their bosses against each of a whole list of management practices and a total rating was produced. A two-day training programme was given in understanding and using the scheme and practising some of the key skill areas. A key results working document is shown in Figure 20.1. Table 20.1 lists examples of the practices identified as essential for a manager to develop in BA (described as performance domains and statements). The review

KEY RESULT AREA PLANNING SHEET   This form to be completed by you and your manager in the regular progress review, and copies held by both. You should inform your manager when each result is achieved, or when issues emerge which might prevent achievement.

Unit Mission (Step 1)

Result Areas (Step 2)	Key results — Major Results to be achieved (Step 3)		Who responsible for specific contributions (Step 4)
	required result, including success criteria	completion date/ priorities	

Figure 20.1   A BA key results working document

Table 20.1 Performance Domains and Statements

STRATEGIC AND BUSINESS AWARENESS

- Develops long-term objectives and plans that are consistent with corporate strategy.
- Creates short-term objectives that fit the strategic framework.
- Predicts long-term implications of short-term actions.
- Promotes means of dealing with ambiguity and uncertainty.
- Communicates effectively the impact of success and failure in own area on the overall business results.
- Demonstrates a wide knowledge of airline activities outside own area.
- Understands BA's customers and their changing needs.
- Takes into consideration external business developments affecting own area.

FLEXIBILITY AND CREATIVITY

- Handles a variety of issues simultaneously.
- Improvises effective solutions when faced by unusual and difficult problems.
- Responds to the need to make decisions under pressure and in difficult situations.
- Quickly acquires knowledge on new subjects when needed.
- Handles conflict and ambiguous situations with resilience.
- Generates creative and practicable ideas.
- Takes responsibility for promoting and implementing new ideas and approaches.

PEOPLE AND TEAM MANAGEMENT

- Morale and motivation of his/her team is high.
- Gets the best out of people, empowers them to exceed regular performance.
- Delegates responsibilities clearly and effectively.
- Holds regular team meetings.
- Shares information with staff about activities and changes affecting their work.
- Stands up for the rights of subordinates when representing them before superiors.
- Praises subordinates' achievements and successes more often than criticizing their faults.
- Recognizes subordinates for innovation and calculated risk taking.

process was a further opportunity for managers to receive feedback from their subordinates.

Pay for performance

The problem of many appraisal systems is individual bias and inconsistency by and between managers. This was reduced by computer analysis of all appraisal data; managers were given feedback on their perceived performance as appraisers. The computer also compared ratings between departments and queried any major differences. It showed halo effects produced by individual managers as well as where too small a part of the rating range was used. On the basis of computer-adjusted results, discussed with senior managers, an element of performance pay was awarded to managers, either on a bonus system for senior managers or variable incremental awards for senior staff. The total amount available was determined by the chief executive and performance appraisal decided the allocation on the basis of unit or team performance as well as individual performance.

A Day in the Life

One successful aspect of PPF was the way it brought staff out of their normal work environment to meet people from other parts of the organization. Colin Marshall was keen to see this happen on a regular basis, and a follow-up to PPF was planned for implementation at the end of 1985. This new programme called A Day in the Life was presented to all BA's staff – now nearing 40,000 – over the following year and also, very successfully, to a number of external audiences. The programme examined, through a number of theme presentations with evocative titles, the way British Airways goes about its business. They were live multi-media presentations, given by managers and staff of the airline. Themes included:

- 'Great Expectations' – about catering and cabin service
- 'Magic of Flight' – the pilots presenting their world
- 'The Golden Touch' – Ground Operations in action
- 'Engineering Excellence' – self explanatory
- 'Money Matters' – the way money works in and for BA

The successes of the past three years were presented in a video called 'Winning Ways', and the day finished with staff giving their views on a topical managerial decision, before questioning Colin Marshall or one of his Executive Team, through the staff host, in a 'hot seat' interview.

Again, this programme illustrated the steadily changing culture within the airline. It was used as a promotional tool with the travel trade and some key customers, and it enhanced the BA image as visitors saw staff presenting their own work enthusiastically and professionally. During the run-up to privatization, the programme was used to introduce the airline to the financial institutions. By the end of the programme, some 500 staff had acted as presenters, with a small team of dedicated staff hosting the whole show. Time Manager International were retained to help train presenters and to monitor programme quality. The actual staging of the programme was carried out by a marketing services company, Purchase-Point, as it involved intricate design and a variety of media to stimulate and interest throughout the day.

Participants received an informative booklet about the airline, with practical information to help promote and sell the airline. The role of staff as ambassadors was seen to be particularly important in the period leading up to privatization.

Both PPF and A Day in the Life improved communication between managers and staff, and a number of local departmental initiatives were established to keep up the momentum and generate new energy. Programmes such as I A D O M (It all depends on me) in Reservations, provided a refresher on standards expected; a focus on service strategy and performance standards was built into the We're Setting the Standards programme for all 6500 staff in Ground Operations London. This programme looked at baggage, cleaning, passenger service and aircraft dispatch, using a punctuality-based aircraft turnround game to create the total picture of service at Heathrow.

As the service model shows, the personal service element concerns the knowledge and skill of the front-line staff, and the attitudes of managers towards customers and their staff are vital ingredients of an effective service strategy. The programmes in this second phase served to develop a firm foundation; the next stage was to ensure the gains were maintained.

21

Holding the gains

In 1983, the Executive Team said that culture change would require a three to five-year campaign. After three years, a noticeable difference had been achieved, commented on by both staff and customers alike. Customer data had continued to play an important part in correcting the strategic course set in 1983, but towards the end of 1986, a comprehensive market research exercise was commissioned to establish changes in perception among customers and among airline management and staff. The findings, produced early in 1987, showed that customers' basic needs had changed little, but their expectations of British Airways' performance had increased. Passengers noted improvements in both material and personal aspects of service, but were still concerned about overall consistency. The research confirmed the messages from the earlier research that passenger goodwill would be created by getting the personal or emotional aspects of service right; that customer loyalty very much depended on their inter-actions with the people of the airline. Internally, there was still concern about the need to drive for both service and quality improvement as well as cost efficiency.

The impending privatization added to the internal uncertainty, but also gave rise to customer doubts; the suspicion was that service improvement might merely be windowdressing for an attractive sale.

Reviewing MPF

These doubts about the future were mirrored in a review by the Human Resources Department to establish the effectiveness of the Managing People First programme and to determine the follow-up requirements of those who attended. The issues to be faced by the management team were also identified, as were views on the cultural change taking place. Not all had liked the programme, but for those who had, the elements of structured feedback and the setting up of support groups had been powerful influences. Those who had disliked the programme had not been comfortable with the changing culture and had found the feedback traumatic or confusing. The majority, however, saw the programme as a clear commitment to uprating managerial competence and recognized that follow-up programmes were required to continue the process of breaking from the traditional bureaucratic, compartmentalized thinking and to make the behaviour change permanent.

It was agreed that an integrated programme of training, covering staff and management, was required to consolidate the progress to date and to reinforce the sense of purpose. There were also specific business needs to be met, which included a better understanding of the competitive framework, improved cross-departmental teamwork, understanding how to exploit information technology and managing change more rapidly.

Globalization was by this time emerging as an inevitable market trend. It was apparent that, within a decade, only a handful of large-scale global operators would still exist. Integrated route networks and flight schedules, supported by powerful distribution systems would be the order of the day. Following the deregulation of the US airline industry, British Airways became the leader in opening up the skies of Europe, a process to be accelerated by the free market of 1992.

Management saw the need to keep a tight rein on costs while continuing to increase the flexibility of staff and to motivate people to address the cross-departmental changes. Management also saw the necessity to constantly review the environment in which the airline operated and the social, political, economic and demographic trends influencing the business. Managers should be trained through the follow-up programmes to recognize the opportunities offered by the dynamic environment and to respond to them in an innovative and entrepreneurial manner.

One final element of this next training phase was a recognition that staff events were now an expectation and a third corporate programme was needed to build on Putting People First and A Day in the Life.

Integrated programme

Three programmes were launched during 1987:

- Leading The Service Business 1 (LSB1) – for the most senior managers
- Leading The Service Business 2 (LSB2) – for the bulk of managers
- To Be The Best – a one-day programme for all staff and managers.

LSB1 was a one-week programme, picking up the main themes of customer service, competition, profitability, technology and speed of decision making. As in the past, attendees were in cross-functional groups and worked mostly in syndicate sessions reviewing the new customer and staff data as well as competitive data. A novel and interesting idea was for some of the customer data to be provided by participants who had to interview a number of customers face-to-face before attending the programme. A climate survey was carried out within each department. employing the same model used to structure the course. The outputs of the course were action plans, relating to the key business issues and the climate surveys, and plans to support LSB2 and To be the Best, including carrying out business briefings to all their managers and staff before the commencement of these programmes.

LSB2 had a much larger target audience and hence took longer. Each programme consisted of two three-day residential programmes, roughly six weeks apart, and management teams attended together – a very important feature. The programme helped management teams with specific issues, such as identifying their customers' needs, comparing performance with competitors, working together, exploiting information technology and gaining the support of their staff. Each team developed its agenda in advance with help from the LSB1 action plans and feedback from To be the Best. Outputs were the evaluation of each team, improvement plans and clearly identified 'partnership' issues between teams.

To be the Best started with a target of 40,000 staff, but this was enlarged by the merger with British Caledonian, who first attended an innovative programme welcoming them to British Airways with a high technology presentation on the lines of A Day in the Life, with the aim of merging cultures as fast as possible. To be the Best built on earlier messages about customer expectations and customer service provision, as well as the teamwork concept. However, the main theme was the growing competitive context facing British Airways. Competitors' strengths were presented by staff teams and their colleagues were asked to develop strategies and tactics to counter these competitor strengths. Customer and competitor research findings were presented, including 'vox pop' feedback from customers. The programme continued the process of seeking continuous improvement in both material and personal aspects of service, reinforced the interdependence of organizational units and brought out staff concerns.

New progammes to develop staff awareness and involvement in the 1990s are presently under discussion.

Other service initiatives

In addition to these integrated corporate initiatives, a number of other service related activities were enhanced or launched to keep the service strategy strong well beyond the five years estimated at the outset.

A regular supply of customer views came through Videobox, a facility offered to passengers at Heathrow who could walk into a booth and record any comment they wished to make. Not statistically meaningful, but nonetheless a rich seam of qualitative data to be tapped, it gave a sense of reality to other customer needs data and also provided opportunities to put things right and generate customer loyalty.

Customer First teams were revitalized; they were asked to revise customer service standards and act more as performance improvement groups.

The interview programme was stepped up to 150,000 per year, providing a regular and reliable source of data to drive the new orientation and to avoid complacency and a return to 'manager knows best' behaviour.

Awards for excellence for 'local heroes' were given at To be the Best, and the Suggestion Scheme was developed to give special recognition to service improvement ideas.

Initiatives continued to be developed to keep the service strategy alive in every front-line unit. These were supported by specific service training, including, for instance, an imaginative interactive video programme called Creating First Impressions for check-in staff, and Serve to Win Everytime for cabin crew.

Finally, to respond to the growing need to listen to customers, regular Customer Forums were set up to debate specific issues with a cross-section of airline customers.

The initiatives continue, the difference has been noticed and the principle of putting the customer first is now definitely part of BA culture. Some £10m has been spent on the corporate initiatives alone. Let's look now at what has been achieved.

Achievements and measuring success

Success should first be measured against the Customer First objectives, described in Chapter 19:

- Staff are convinced about satisfying customer needs
- Standards exist for customer service
- Customer monitoring takes place regularly
- Data from the latter showed a large increase in customer satisfaction early in the programme and confirms that these gains have been held since
- Staff are convinced about service and involved in its improvement
- Monitoring of front-line staff takes place regularly against clear standards
- There is a faster internal response to problems.

None of the above areas is perfect, but collectively they demonstrate substantial progress and show that the service strategy has made an impact, both in the marketplace and in the way the company is run. Staff understand the rationale for change and operate at a micro level (the customer interface) in a way which is compatible with the macro, more strategic work of the senior team.

Successful privatization in 1987 confirmed the progress and in 1988/9 revenue was more than double that of 1983. Growth and profitability have been reflected in share performance since the flotation. 94 per cent of staff took the opportunity to buy BA shares at flotation time, much of their funding coming from profit share trusts that had been developed over the previous three years.

Acknowledged now as one of the world's most profitable airlines, BA represents a classic case of new management methods and attitudes rebuilding a service company to become a leader in a competitive and increasingly global market. As an example of a service strategy which has worked, it demonstrates the amount of effort required, the range of improvement activities which have to be initiated and the number of people who have to be involved.

As Colin Marshall said:

'It is our intention to be the best airline in the world; quality of service is paramount. This means 'Putting the Customer First' in everything we do.'

Summary of Part III

British Airways achieved real change, sustained over a long period, by creative effort and hard work. The chief components of success were:

- Establishing base research and then mechanisms for regular capture of customer need and performance data
- Setting a clear common purpose
- Using customer data to set service standards to generate service improvement
- Recognizing the need for awareness programmes for all staff at regular intervals
- Setting up and supporting team mechanisms and tapping potential at all levels of the organization
- Investing in substantial corporate management training programmes and linking this to performance appraisal and performance pay
- Using service improvement in a considered way as a marketing tool
- Being innovative with service initiatives, but keeping within a coherent strategic framework.

Conclusions: pitfalls and payoffs

We have seen how a service strategy can be built based on data on your marketplace and an organizational vision. The strategic model shows that the strategy must cover every aspect of the organization and it helps you judge the size of the task ahead. The task is outlined and then converted into a coherent action plan – a framework of communication, training, improvement and monitoring activities designed to achieve and maintain a new responsiveness to your customers. The British Airways story illustrated the long-term nature of changing a culture from operational to market led and as a result, creating a prosperous and growing organization with a sustained reputation for quality of service.

Now, hopefully, you are in no doubt that developing a customer-led, quality-conscious approach in your own organization can pay dividends. Creating service as a key strategic value, listening to your customers and responding in a way that pleases them can have lasting benefits. The aim of the programmes described in this book is to make 'customer first' behaviour a way of life by building a climate where continuous improvement in quality and innovation is natural and where the concept of the internal customer is a comfortable one for everybody in the organization.

None of this is achieved easily, it requires a long-term commitment and much effort in order for the difference to be noticed by your critical external and internal audiences. Yet your very survival may depend on making these changes. In addition to this perhaps rather threatening scenario there are positive benefits if you can overcome the many hurdles and pitfalls. A clear idea of what your organization will feel and look like will enable you to plan, and give inspiration when problems occur, while helping you to gauge progress. In this last section I'd like to emphasize the benefits of becoming customer oriented. First, I will briefly indicate the main hurdles and pitfalls which may occur and describe some ways of anticipating and avoiding them while providing a motivating picture of how your organization could look different as a result.

Hurdles and pitfalls

It is certain that there will be many hurdles in your way and means have to be found to avoid or circumnavigate them. There will also be unexpected pitfalls which will have to be coped with. Using the experiences of others can help you to anticipate and perhaps to avoid some of them – so talk to other people, attend conferences, read books, transfer learning wherever it is going to be helpful.

Customer First is creating change in a real and lasting way. There will be many areas of resistance to overcome; to you these may appear to be based on illogical, irrational and emotional thinking. Just as with convincing customers to buy, people within the organization have to be motivated to 'buy-in', so these perceptions cannot be ignored, however difficult they may be for you to accept or understand. People facing change can undergo a whole series of negative emotions – anger, denial, frustration and at best resignation. All of these have to be countered if you are seeking enthusiastic, fearless commitment to change. Resistance may be to do with having change imposed, rather than the change itself. Allowing people to become involved in defining the nature of the change required and the subsequent processes for its implementation will remove much of the resistance. People must be allowed to let go of their old ways of doing things in a manner which maintains their self esteem. If you wish them to be a part of the new culture, bridges with their past have to be built. Although people often resist prescribed change there will need to be some – new structures, specific techniques, carefully chosen projects, improvement targets etc. Therefore time has to be taken to help people understand a reason to accept these changes. Customer First or total quality cannot be achieved by system improvements alone. People change systems and as such their enthusiasm and commitment have to be won.

One obvious pitfall is not having a sufficiently coherent, well thought out framework of activities, which are multi-faceted and so work together to bring about the improvements required. As the Japanese are renowned for saying – 'long on planning, short on implementation', a maxim which can serve you well.

A further pitfall is not recognizing the need to have a critical mass of believers and enthusiasts with organizational influence, either in the formal structure or the informal networks which are part of any organization. Critical mass is not an absolute number but the number required to give impetus and maintain momentum and will be different according to the stage of the change programme. By use of these enthusiasts your programme activities can start by convincing the persuadable neutrals who constitute the bulk of most normal populations.

The biggest hurdle is often the middle management group, waiting for repeated signals of commitment from the top or contra signals and mixed messages which allow them to stay neutral. Blaming the attitudes of their workforce for quality problems, being threatened by the changing nature of their role, feeling increasingly isolated and fearful of the future are all characteristic behaviours; and they can be quietly and insidiously undermining progress. This particular hurdle can only be overcome by persistent leadership from the senior team providing clear championing of 'customer first' and role modelling quality behaviour. By their investment decision they show their overt support for meeting customer needs with quality goods and services. Management training is an essential contributor to allow managers the time to debate, become committed and acquire the new skills required.

Other aspects which will soon undermine the programme, if not anticipated, are:

- Failure to start with improvement projects which are likely to be successful; teams soon get dispirited if they don't achieve success, and success in the early projects breeds confidence and hence more success
- Becoming complacent and as a result not retaining the gains or seeking further opportunities for improvement
- Becoming stale after a few months as enthusiasm begins to drop. All programmes will meet peaks and troughs of enthusiasm and progress. Be prepared with some new ideas, new champions and the odd surprise to keep people alert; keep the successes visible, use data constantly to renew energy levels
- Managers not listening – either to customers or employees. 'Manager knows best' behaviour is always lurking, ready to resume control at the least opportunity. Listening to customers and staff means you are constantly challenging your thinking and testing your ideas. Listening is also the biggest respect you can pay to people while it also provides you with data. Its absence will be the biggest signal to the organization of your lack of commitment to improvement.

What it will feel like

As we discussed on p.19, a vision is needed of what your organization could look and feel like when the cultural change has been achieved. The concept of continuous improvement and changing marketplaces will ensure that it is a continuous journey you are undertaking with no final destination. However, we have talked about achieving a noticeable difference and we must be able to express how this difference might be perceived – both from an external and internal point of view. The following are some indicators of customer progress, although not all will be equally applicable to all organizations. Your own vision work will indicate which are of more relevance to your company.

Externally
- Customers see the company as:
  - responsive to their needs; good listeners

147

- adding value through innovative products and services
- sharing data and taking part in joint problem solving, generally seeking a partnership approach
- recognizing the importance of third party accreditation in creating customer confidence
- understanding the customer's business and the factors critical to their success
- caring about the way they deal with each customer
- Competitors see the company as formidable
- Shareholders regard the company as a safe, worthwhile investment
- The communities within which the company exists see it as a caring partner, concerned for the social and economic environment
- Future potential employees see the company as one they would be proud to work for

Internally
- Style of operation is characterized by:
  - service and quality is part of every routine meeting and influences every decision
  - systematic, data driven approaches to problem solving involve everyone; and are visibly displayed
  - problems are seen as opportunities, root causes are identified and problems rarely recur

- Staff investment is reflected by:
  - people are valued, trust abounds and personal recognition and reward occur naturally
  - employees are proud of their work, their colleagues and their company and actively promote the virtues of the company
  - training is readily available and eagerly sought by everyone for both job and personal development
  - everybody knows their customers; and what is expected of them by their customers

- Management behaviour is based on:
  - visionary and overt leadership, clearly championing service quality improvement and leading by example
  - setting clear priorities and targets
  - creating a climate for continuous improvement, role modelling improvement by learning and practising new techniques; carefully choosing improvement projects for others to be involved in
  - listening to staff, responding to ideas non defensively, using coaching as a means of problem solving
  - breaking down barriers to get problems solved rather than protecting territory; sharing information openly not using it as a power source

Benefits

The vision of what can be achieved is exciting – it really can be a different place to work and a different company to do business with. There are many opportunities for stumbling and failing but with care these can be overcome or avoided. The question is 'Is it all going to be worth it?' Whilst the question can be avoided by showing that there is no choice if you want to become or remain competitive, there are also many positive, certain benefits to provide an affirmative answer to the question. Hard benefits which make a contribution to the growth and prosperity of the company are:

- Guaranteed service quality becomes a marketable product in itself with a price differential acceptable to customers
- Quality improvement provides a cost effective organization since waste, re-work and compensation become a thing of the past
- A common purpose and alignment removes ineffective training and compartmentalization and generates trust and enthusiasm
- A better educated, more numerate management and workforce are better prepared to face and handle change confidently and without fear, including market downturns; change becomes welcomed and sought after; cries for stability disappear
- Management systems and processes are uprated and the climate of continuous improvement ensures they are regularly reviewed for effectiveness, amended or removed
- Energy and potential are released at all levels to create an altogether more powerful, innovative and more responsive organization
- Partnership programmes ensure only the best suppliers are kept and effort on new business generation is reduced as growth comes from customer loyalty and mutual development.

Customer First is a state of mind producing an organization which is customer led. Quality and safety-conscious, concerned for the development of its people and as a result:

Highly Successful

The journey is worthwhile and enjoyable.

The destination is worth aspiring to.

The pay-off is immense.

Index